Children Using Language

An approach to English in the primary school

Edited by
Anthony Jones and
Jeremy Mulford

CHILDREN USING LANGUAGE

Children Using Language

*An approach to English
in the primary school*

Edited by
Anthony Jones and Jeremy Mulford

Published for the
NATIONAL ASSOCIATION FOR THE TEACHING
OF ENGLISH

by the Oxford University Press: 1971

Oxford University Press, Ely House,
London W.1

GLASGOW NEW YORK TORONTO MELBOURNE
WELLINGTON CAPE TOWN SALISBURY IBADAN
NAIROBI DAR ES SALAAM LUSAKA
ADDIS ABABA BOMBAY CALCUTTA MADRAS
KARACHI LAHORE DACCA KUALA LUMPUR
SINGAPORE HONG KONG TOKYO

This book is the result of one part
of a project on 'Language in the
Primary School', carried out by the
National Association for the Teaching
of English in conjunction with the
Calouste Gulbenkian Foundation, whose
financial assistance we gratefully acknowledge.

Printed in Great Britain by
Northumberland Press Ltd., Gateshead

CONTENTS

CONTRIBUTORS

James Nimmo Britton

is Professor of Education at Goldsmith's College, University of London. He has broadcast in the B.B.C. Poetry series *Adventures in English*, and the TV programme, 'First Foundations', in the series *Mother Tongue*. Publications include: *The Oxford Books of Verse for Juniors* (O.U.P.), *The Oxford Books of Stories for Juniors* (O.U.P), *Talking and Writing* (Editor) (Methuen), and *Language and Learning* (Allen Lane). Prof. Britton is Chairman of the National Association for the Teaching of English.

Ian Burton

is Lecturer in English and Drama at Newton Park College of Education. He has had experience of Drama in schools and Arts Centres, and in the professional theatre in Toronto and Chichester.

*Winifred Fawcus

is Senior Staff Tutor at the University of Newcastle, Institute of Education, in charge of the full-time course for the Diploma of Advanced Educational Studies (Primary). She has previously taught in Primary and Secondary Schools and in a Froebel College of Education.

*Anthony Jones

is Head of the English Department at Newton Park College of Education. Previously, he taught in Secondary Modern and Grammar Schools, although his initial training was for Primary teaching. Publications include: *Dan Berry's New Baby* (Blackie), *Dan Berry Goes to Hospital* (Blackie) and (with June Buttrey) *Children and Stories*

(Blackwell, 1971). Mr. Jones is Chairman of N.A.T.E.'s Primary Schools Sub-Committee.

*Nancy C. Martin

is Senior Lecturer in the University of London Institute of Education, Division of Language Teaching. She is especially concerned with Research into the development of writing abilities, and with Advanced Diplomas in Language and Education. Publications include: 'The Multiple Marking of English Compositions' (with James Britton and Harold Rosen) in Schools Council *Examinations Bulletin* No. 12; *Oxford English Source Books* (O.U.P.): *Here, Now and Beyond, Truth to Tell*, and *Half-Way*; and 'Stages of Progress in Language' in *Talking and Writing* (ed. James Britton) (Macmillan). Miss Martin is Secretary of Studies to the London Association for the Teaching of English, and was Chairman of the L.A.T.E. Committee that produced *Assessing Compositions* (Blackie).

*Jeremy Mulford

is Director of the N.A.T.E./Schools Council Project, 'Children as Readers'. He has taught mainly in Primary Schools; but also in a Day College, a University, a College of Education, and in Adult Education. With Gavin Edwards, he edits *Partizan*.

*Connie Rosen

is Director of the Schools Council Project, 'Language Development in the Primary School', on secondment from the University of London Goldsmiths' College, where she works in teacher training on the Three-year course and the One-year Postgraduate Primary Course. Previously, she taught in Primary Schools in Middlesex and Hertfordshire. Publications include: contributions to N.A.T.E.'s *Primary English*, Brian Jackson's *English versus Examinations* (Chatto and Windus) and James Britton's *Talking and Writing* (Methuen).

8

Margaret Spencer

is Lecturer in English in the University of London Institute of Education. She is also Reviews Editor of *The School Librarian*. Publications include: two Bodley Head Monographs, *Geoffrey Trease* and *Rosemary Sutcliff*.

In addition to the contributors marked with an asterisk above, the following were members of N.A.T.E.'s Primary Schools Sub-Committee while this book was being produced: —

Bernard Bryan, College of Education Lecturer and N.A.T.E.'s Secretary of Studies

John Coe, Senior Adviser for Primary Education to the Oxfordshire Education Committee

Joan Dean, General Adviser for Primary Education, Berkshire

Eric Finney, Primary School Head Teacher

John Hird, College of Education Lecturer and Secretary to the Comittee

Ralph Lavender, Primary School Head and Schools Library Association representative

Tony Perry, College of Education Lecturer

Geoffrey Romans, H.M.I.

Harold Stephenson, Senior Assistant Education Officer, Staffordshire

Dan Taverner, Primary Schools Adviser and Treasurer to the Committee

Sheila Tennent, Junior School Teacher

Lilian Thompson, Infant School Head

Ruth Walker, Primary School Head

N.A.T.E.'s Primary Schools Sub-Committee has also been responsible for the following publications: —

    English in the Primary School (the Association's evidence to the Plowden Committee)
    Primary English (N.A.T.E. Bulletin, Vol. 3, No. 3), edited by John Hird

INTRODUCTION

In October 1966, the National Association for the Teaching of English received a grant from the Calouste Gulbenkian Foundation 'to examine the future of Primary School Teaching in the light of the Plowden Report, and to produce positive and constructive recommendations to guide future developments'. The Plowden Report was published early in 1967, and soon afterwards a working party of N.A.T.E.'s Primary Schools Sub-Committee produced the following recommendations:

1. Not to produce a general report similar in kind to *English in the Primary School*, or a document recording actual teaching such as *Primary English*; but instead,
2. To study the place of language in the life and growth of young children, and produce a report on this.
3. Recognizing that talk is the most significant mode of language in the lives of young children, to set up study groups to produce material that would help teachers to a greater awareness of this fact.

As a result of the latter recommendation, groups centred on the Staffordshire branches of N.A.T.E. have collected tapes of children talking in all kinds of situations; and these are being transcribed and edited as material for loan to teachers' courses, etc., and perhaps for general publication. This book is the result of the second recommendation.

At a later date, the Primary Sub-Committee laid plans for a seminar to study children's early reading experience, and the implications of this for the development of teaching methods and the provision of materials. This seminar took place in October 1970, and it is intended that it should be followed up by further meetings between teachers, writers and editors.

11

After studying and discussing the Plowden Report, the Primary Sub-Committee decided to ask James Britton to write an article, based on a talk given to one of its Summer Schools, offering an account of language which could act as the starting-point for a series of other articles. This was circulated and discussed among all the intending contributors to the symposium, as well as other members of the Committee, who supplied school material that is drawn on in some of the articles.

We should make it clear that this symposium does not attempt to be comprehensive; and neither does any article attempt to deal comprehensively with its particular topic. However, the fact that the contributors share a number of basic premises should give the book a coherence. The functions of the editorial comment are to emphasize this, and to set the book, in some measure, in the context of other recent work on English teaching by supplementing contributors' references.*

The book opens with a descriptive prelude.

---

* For a short, personal account of developments in thinking about English in the Primary School during the last thirty years or so, see Jeremy Mulford, 'The Primary School', in Denys Thompson (Ed.), *Directions in the Teaching of English* (C.U.P.).

OBJECT LESSON

Connie Rosen

Linda from the top class arrived in my classroom with a tin. Tins were always arriving for savings moneys, collections for departing staff or lost pennies. This one contained a message that the Inspector had arrived. His car number, chalked on the door of the caretaker's 'office' (that is the boiler room), had been noted as it came down the drive, and every member of staff knew that he'd arrived by the time his car had come to a halt and he'd opened the door. Only a drum beat could have been speedier or more efficient.

By the time he arrived in my classroom we were doing the Normans. He smiled, looked round and asked me why I was doing the Normans. I said it was an interesting story. His glasses looked at me, the floor, the ceiling, I tried again. I said small boys seemed to enjoy the military tactics and there had been several revised versions of Hastings in the playground. He fidgeted. It was clear he wasn't at all happy. I tried again. The Bayeux Tapestry was very colourful. We had reproduced it in the same colours. No response. I resorted to cultural heritage and it being an important thing for children to have like fresh air and milk. It was obvious that he'd given up trying to get me to think at all critically about the business so he turned to the children. He began asking them questions like dates and how long ago it had all happened and whether their grandparents had been there and what country the Normans had come from, none of which could they answer. It was just as well it wasn't the era of payment by results. I shouldn't have earned enough for a packet of tea.

The staff room was a little warm after the departure of the Inspector. He'd visited classes with needlework and classes of P.T. and it had all come to the same thing. We protested. We were indignant. We capped each others' stories of his enigmatic manner. We had examples of the way he'd thrown different children into confusion though

13

it was clear that it was really we who were perplexed. And anyway the Headmaster was being too friendly. It wasn't the way to go on with Inspectors. He'd made him feel he could just drop in at any time for cups of tea and little chats. But somewhere, somehow he'd left doubt, a feeling that things weren't quite right, that perhaps we ought to think again, that perhaps we could do better.

We did think again. We agreed at a staff meeting to do a local study. Somebody wanted the woods, somebody wanted fathers' occupations, somebody wanted a scale model, somebody wanted the drainage and water works and things like that and I took the buildings.

My class of nine-year-olds and I began with the 500-year-old Tithe Barn. We walked through leafy woods one sunny morning and the children chattered, picked flowers, ran and stopped, gathered round and strung out again. When we arrived, the massive scale of timbers and rafters and roof astonished them. They paced out the great doorway we'd been told was wide enough for a loaded cart of hay to pass through. Andrew and Graham had brought their rulers. In fact they never went on any of our trips without them, though the rulers had more to do with their own desire for precision and accuracy than with anything we actually needed to measure. The children examined the wooden pegs in the rafters: they stood on the twelve-inch boards of the threshing floor, crowded round the farmer's tractor and hung over the calves in the stalls. They looked at the flint-embedded walls, and Paul was pleased when one of the flints fell on his toe so that we could take it back and say we had a Tottenhoe flint from the Tithe Barn. The farmer and his son stoically continued their work while the children seemed to be in every corner of stall and surrounding grounds and farmhouse. They photographed each other in front of Barn and house, measured and wrote, felt and observed, asked questions and made sketches.

Back in the classroom, I listened to their comments and measurements. Their pictures of the barn, the tithe collecting and the threshing had an Anglo-Saxon flavour. I did some homework and discovered that we had once

14

belonged to the manor of Canterbury and then later to two Oxford colleges.

Mary wrote:

On Thursday we went to have a look round the Tithe Barn. We went through the woods and we saw a grey squirrel which jumped from a branch to a very thick branch. The trees were not all out, but the flowers were. The Tithe Barn is on Cupfield Hall Farm. The outside of the barn is made of flint and stone, and the tiles are very uneven. A lot of the barn is the arridginal material. At the tops of the roof there were nests, the tiles had moss and grass growing on them. There were holes in the roof. It was very dark in there. The walls are made of oak wood, which in colour were grey and white. Inside there were some cows. One cow's name was called Daisy, another Diana and the last one was called Susan. One cow licked my hand. The floor is made of wood and concrete, the part where it is concrete was once earth. After that we went to have a look at six baby calfs. When we went home we went through the woods again. On the way I picked some flowers and leaves.

We next went to the Windmill, and did what everybody does with windmills, walked round and round it. We gazed down the hollow gate post at the blue tit's nest and found several old mill stones propped up around the mill and being used as steps and paving stones. We felt them, took rubbings of their surfaces and stood on them to take possession of them. We peered through the cobwebby windows and discovered the remains of the platform from which the miller had once tended the sails. The following day Colin tottered to school with an encyclopaedia half as big as himself. He'd been carrying out his own investigations. He showed us pictures of two kinds of windmills and explained the construction of Dutch Mills and Post Mills. It was clear that ours was a Dutch Mill as there wasn't a top half that swivelled round separately. He then went on to explain that our mill had once had two sets of stones, one for coarse flour and one for fine. 'What is coarse flour?' asked Alan, so we talked about all the different kinds of bread we'd ever eaten, and then went on to think about butter and jam and honey and tea-time until we were all hungry. (I was reminded of the occasion when with a different group of children we'd made some bread and the Headmaster who'd looked in on the kneading being done on the rota system had commented that it was a good thing that the bread was brown, and that fire was a great purifier.) We had a Miller and a Milne in the classroom so their ancestors must have known all about mills and milling. It had also been a great challenge to the photographers in the class to get the whole mill into a photograph and a couple did actually manage it without giving it either a Pisa slope or with the top chopped off which had marked my own efforts. Graham and Vicki wrote:

On Friday we went to look at the old mill. We had to go up a long drive to get to the windmill itself. When we got up there two dogs came scattering out and started to bark at the gate, but the lady came and fetched them in. So after that we walked down the garden of Windmill House to the windmill. It had very small bricks with a small house to the south of it and a shed to the west of it. The sails have been taken off, and there were pieces of iron round it where there had been a platform to fix the sails if they went wrong. It has arch windows. On the door there is a wooden bar. The top looks like an old shade. There was a millstone in front of the mill door. It is about a hundred years old. There are stinging nettles growing on the mill as well as ivy and a yew tree growing on it. There are chickens in the windmill.

Jenny said that her daddy said that the pub, 'The Four in Hand', had once been a coaching inn and that there were old coaching stables at the back, and she brought a painting she'd done at home of a coach and four to prove it. So off we went to have a look. Amidst the strong tang of spirits and beer, that made me somewhat uneasy, the children went from stuffed fox and pheasant to lioness and looked up the wide chimney at the sky. They found an old coach lantern, a bell under the eaves and a disused well. They wanted to know how old the hollow tree was, noticed the little bricks in the chimney and I wondered what the lioness's head and stuffed animals and the smell of drink had to do with our study. Bobby saved the day by remarking that the timber work was called post and something, wasn't it? And my teacher's conscience produced some hasty talk about post and pan work.

Dennis, knowing nothing of teachers' consciences, but knowing better, wrote:

'The Four-in-Hand' was the best of all. We went inside the stables and there were about five deer head, a lioness's head, 1 leopard head, a Fish's head and a stuffed fox with a pheasant. I looked right up the chimney. It was a very big one. The fireplace was about three times as big as ours today. Under the rafters hung a bell which travellers used to ring and the landlord had to come out. The rope is cut short, but you can imagine it being long.

Some of the children wrote pieces on their own or friends' houses. Anything built before 1930 seemed old to them. Elizabeth wrote:

'Briars' was built in 1860. It has a well under the lawn and a pump. There is a cellar where the Tussauds used to make wax works. The Tussauds are quite famous for their work and they used to wash their hands so they did not have to keep running up and down stairs. There are eight bells, one is for the front door, one for the back and the other six are used in the bedrooms so if they were ill all they had to do was pull a cord and

17

the maid in the kitchen would hear it and come and see what you would like. There was an old-fashioned hearth. After they had died some other people came.

Nicola was alarmingly efficient and she wrote about her grandfather's tiny Tudor cottage on the Green. Grandfather and Nicola had had a fine old time making the inventory. No detail of its construction was omitted from her two foolscap sheets:

The latches on the doors have a piece of straight wood that you can lift up and down and then just below the piece of wood there is a hole in the door, so if you were outside you would have to put your finger through the hole and then push up the latch. The old door frames are not planed. They are just a tree trunk stuck to the wall....

Timothy went to see his friends who lived in the Vicarage. He drew a plan of it and brought some leaves from its strange Gingko tree. I'd never heard of one before and read it all up in an encyclopaedia. The botanical details all seemed too complicated either for the children or me, but we liked the bit about it having originated in the Temple gardens in China and that it dated from Jurassic times when other trees had been turning into coal. We pressed the heart-shaped leaves, mounted them and made some prints from them. Graham mostly liked trains so he wrote about the railway station. Carol asked her Grandad about the Mill and brought picture postcards of when it had been burnt down. Alan brought his account of the Church in four stages. He began with the Church Hall. Then he found a postcard of the window. Then he made a list of the Vicars. Then he wrote about being in the Church Choir and the different rates for Sundays, weddings and christenings. I was interested to discover that the Church had been built in the nineteenth century on a corner of the Green, and the details of how a piece of common land had been acquired for this purpose were related to friends and family.

We looked at the Sarsen Stone and Shirley wrote:

> In the churchyard of St. John's Church we saw a sarsen stone. It was like a rock. Stone age man used it for marking roads (rough tracks). It is very old.

Stones did keep occurring as we went around. We kept finding a very smooth, brown stone used in one or two places for cobbles and a geological son informed me that it was Hertfordshire pudding stone. We picked up one weighing 7lb. 4oz. and carried it back to the classroom with us where it stayed for a long time being weighed, stroked, used as a paper weight, a door stopper and a clay mould. We discovered that the area had been in fact the furthermost tip of the ice cap and that lots and lots of smoothed and varied stones had been left around and one of the dads on hearing this piece of information sent back to say that he knew, they were all in his garden.

We were next going to visit Birchill Farm. On our way there we passed the public house where the children said the parrot swore at you and where the first local Mutual Aid Society had been started. We looked at the house where once the eccentric Joey had kept his coffin under his bed for forty years. They gazed at the quiet sunny house, pleased with the macabre note, and disappointed that neither the cross he'd tied to the tree nor the coffin were any longer to be seen. 'Why did he do it?' they asked. Why indeed? I didn't know. You can talk about objects much more easily than the vagaries of human beings to children. It was like the question Janet had once asked about Robin Hood and Joan of Arc. She said that if Robin Hood had been a bad man and an outlaw, why did we now think he was good, and that if Joan of Arc was a good person why had they burnt her?

However, we arrived at Birchill Farm and the farmer took them six at a time to look inside the house. They picked their way across polished floors and between armchairs and china ornaments. We looked at the swallows' nests in the garage shed and at the windows that had to be left open for them when they arrived. If the farmer was too late in opening the windows the swallows all sat in a row along the wall waiting for him to come.

Bobby wrote:

> On Wednesdays we went to Birchill Farm and we went in Mr. Gardner's house. There was a very old chimney that the chimney sweep had to climb up to sweep it. There were big iron struts that the boy had to climb up. So we went with Mr. Gardner upstairs. They were very small and low. Upstairs in the bedroom the floorboards are about one foot wide. Soon we went to see the barn. Mr. Gardner said the ships' timbers had to be on the sea about five hundred years before they were broken up to make barns and the landowner would buy the timber to make a barn. He would have timbers taken to him. It would take a very long time to get to him. Mr. Gardner said that he thought the barn's timbers were in the war because when they were making a door they found a bullet. There is a cherry ladder that they used for swinging from one tree to another. If it fell he would have to buy the beer for the others. But the cherry ladder is not used now because they do not let the trees grow so big. In his garage he had some swallows' nests, but some of them have nothing in. He has a blackbird's nest in the brambles in the house. Also he has a spotted fly catcher's nest in a gate of one shed. He did have a blackbird's nest in a rubber tube in another tool shed, but he took it out.

There was something special about our visit to the eighteenth-century house that was being used as an old people's home. We couldn't go into the house but we were allowed to look at the well at the back of the house. No one else in the school had known about it, not even the locals on the staff. It was as though we were the first to discover it. There were of course dozens of disused wells in the area and we kept coming across them in our travels, but this one had been much more elaborately constructed with platform and wheels and cover. What interested everyone was how it worked, where you stood, why it was constructed in that way. It didn't take long for some of them to realize the arrangement of wheels was similar to the gears on bicycles. Timothy eventually made a Meccano model of the well with help from an interested dad who was taken along to see it, and the arrangement of chain, bucket and geared wheels was carefully explained to the others.

Elizabeth wrote:

> The well is two hundred and fifty years old. It is a
> big one with a roof so that when they had to
> get water and it was raining they would not get wet.
> There is a big wheel and a little one underneath.
> If you turn the big wheel once the little one would
> go round many times. There is a little wheel beside
> the big one with spikes on it where the chain
> was fitted on. The water bucket was a very big
> barrel at the side. There was a bench for the
> person to stand on when they were turning the
> wheel. There was some wood over the hole, but
> we were not to stand on it because it was not very
> strong.

We wrote many thank-you letters after our visits. But they weren't merely dutiful of the squeezed-out post birthday variety. In one to the farmer Jenny enquired anxiously after the dog's health, 'for', she said, 'I would hate it if he was ill'. And David wrote:

> Dear Mr. Gardner,
> I liked the visit very much. I took four nice
> photographs. I liked going in the old house very
> much. I felt as if I was there years ago looking
> out of the window at the people going into the
> barn. I think I liked the barn best with the six

foxes' tails and the nice smell of the straw. I liked
the dog with its nice warm coat. I saw the swallow's
nest at the back of the garage. I enjoyed the little
talks you gave, and I saw the cherry ladder as well.

For me, the most dramatic experience of all was a
book not a building. By the time people were beginning
to wonder why we were always crossing the Green, we
were ready to listen to Miss Collins back in the classroom and sedately in our desks. She is the headmistress
of our neighbouring Infants' School, and came to give us
a talk about its history. And its history was tucked under
her arm. It was in a big black book, the Log Book of her
school going back over fifty years. She propped it on my
desk and read some of it to us, snippets about bad attend-
ance when it was too hot, too cold or too wet, when the
children hadn't got boots to come to school or were
helping in the fields, boxes of letters for building words
(1896), the live hedgehog (1895), the live parrot (1897)
and the first nature walk (1911). I wondered what my
nine year olds would make of it all, and when Miss
Collins had gone we looked at the minute hemming on
the needlework samples. The children pored over the
Log Book with its funny writing and 'S's' like 'F's'. I said
I could remember using slates and slate pencils when I
was at school, but Susan said her mummy had used pencils
and paper, whereupon Colin wanted to know why some
had slates and some pencils. Gaynor asked whether Miss
Collins had been talking about schools in the Middle
Ages. We thought about Jane's Grandad, who'd come in
to see us the previous day, and how old he was, and
decided with the help of blackboard and chalk that he
was four years old when the school had begun and could
have been in the babies' class. They collected dates and
details like squirrels. They decided the children had been
very squashed, but that there had been some compen-
sations in the school's history such as when there had
been no teacher for the babies for three months, and when
the windows had been smashed in the blitz so that everyone had had a holiday.

22

Barbara wrote:

On Thursday Miss Collins came along to give us
a little talk about the school when it was first
built in 1875. She told us when the infant room
was built. In 1894 there were a hundred and ninety-
six babies in one room with only one headmistress
to cope with them. In the beginning the children
started school under three. Then they decided to
send home all the children under five in 1911.
The parents had to pay fees of a penny or two for
the education. When free education came in 1891
more pupils came. The war came and the school
was bombed and all the windows were broken. In
1896 the first papers and pencils were got for the
pupils for the first time. In 1895 the first photo
was taken. And in 1897 the backs were put on
the gallery seats. In 1909 there was the first medical
inspection. 1922 there was the first Christmas
party. All these things are put down in the log
book. In 1929 the parents visited the school to see
the children's work. The boys began to knit in 1891.

Janis wrote:

Miss Collins left the log book with us so that we
could have a look. There is old English writing
in the log book such as 'the discipline and progrefs
of the children deserves praise.' Progress is spelt
differently. Miss is spelt M-i-f-s. In object lessons
they had to write about things that were written
down on the blackboard, such as cow, rabbit,
sponge, balloon, lamp, Ascot Races, to make the
children intelligent. They would write a sentence
for each—Cow—A cow is a thing which gives us
milk, or, A cow's babies are called calves.

The log book is very interesting. Boys were to do
things girls did, but girls did pricking and needlework.
The children had slates and slate pencils. They sharpened
their pencils on a wall outside the school.

23

The log book contained for me a glimpse of the history of infant education but the interest the children took in all the minute details surprised me. It is so easy to underestimate children—their concentration and capacity to learn.

A child had recently joined the school who had provoked a great deal of discussion and reminiscences of childhood in the staff room. It was partly her appearance, the woollen coat that was just too long and worn on days that did not warrant a thick coat, a woollen cap that was warm but not very pretty; but it was mainly her air, a lack of confidence, a withdrawal from other children and new experiences that seemed to provoke the reminiscences more than anything else. There we sat and indulged ourselves thinking of early years spent in a Welsh mining valley, on a Suffolk farm, in a Hertfordshire village and in the East End of London. It made a pleasant change from the five minutes' reminiscences we allowed each of the men on the staff from time to time of their military exploits in war time. It all had little to do with Ruth, but we were surprised and pained by her isolation in the midst of the happy, confident children who enjoyed what she lacked, a stability at home and school, and we wanted to understand and explain it.

Somehow in the course of our examination of the Log Book it all came together. I remembered the tiled buildings up which one ascended from babies to big girls, the stepped classroom, the weekly drawing lesson of the daffodil or the cone and, once, a piece of cherry blossom with wrinkled and shiny reddish bark. It was true there had been innumerable mysterious brown boxes containing coloured sticks and counters and letters, and a moment of despair and panic as I looked at the word on the blackboard and was convinced that I was never, never going to read. There was somebody in a floral overall who sat at the front in needlework lessons embroidering a beige princess slip. She seemed very remote and as difficult to understand as the strange garment she sewed —and what a secret and shaming thought to think of her putting it on! But there they all met, Ruth, our own childhood, the story of Infant Schools in the Log Book and the children who had consumed the whole venture with such interest and curiosity and enthusiasm. They'd spent the time enquiring into the buildings, their history, the materials, weighed and measured, talked and written, drawn and painted, and taken the whole lot in their stride. Gingko trees, wild flowers and birds' nests, windmills and gear wheels, Tithe Barn and Ascot Races. Perhaps my predecessor had found life more peaceful, though 196 children in one room took some thinking about. I was grateful to the teacher of the Log Book and remembered her with affection, but I closed her Log Book with relief.

The children in Connie Rosen's class talked and wrote about their experiences: they did not set out at any time to do 'creative writing'. The issue of making creative writing a special (sometimes time-tabled) activity will be taken up at several places in this book.

Mrs. Rosen's article describes a particular class of children at work with their teacher during a particular period of time. James Britton now presents tools with which we can analyse and evaluate children's use of language, and our own teaching.

WORDS AND A WORLD

James Britton

As human beings we cannot escape the influence of language. It pervades all we do: the activities of every waking hour bear its stamp and it shapes more or less directly the material of our dreams. Perhaps it is principally for this reason that we find it as difficult to answer the question, 'What do we use our language for?' as we would to satisfy the child who says, 'What are people for?'.

We might catalogue situations and kinds of utterance and try to give a particular answer as to what each is for —small talk at the tea party, chat in the launderette, the sermon on Sunday, a monograph on lepidoptera, or Keats' 'Ode to a Grecian Urn'. But what would the answers have in common? What major features would shape an answer to the *general* question?

More promising perhaps to consider what effect language has upon a young child's behaviour when first he acquires the ability to use it. The small child who learns to speak begins to live in a new way. Hitherto, all that he has done has been a contribution to the family activities, its corporate existence; now he begins to contribute more of what he *is* than what he *does* could reveal. But, to feel the justice of the claim that he 'begins to live in a new way', we have to think not of the family's point of view but of the child's; and from his point of view, this contribution of himself through speaking bears the aspect of 'becoming' rather than of 'revealing'. In speaking he *discovers* more of what he is than he could discover in action. And since he has at first no inner dialogue with which to operate, all this discovery, this 'becoming', is spoken aloud for all to hear.

The change does not, of course, take place overnight. In the course of a year or eighteen months, two notable stages mark its progress. The first is the discovery that things have names, and that this is a fact about the world —in other words that *everything* may be assumed to have a name. Most children at this stage play what has been called 'the naming game', but is perhaps more usually a 'touching and naming game'. Here is the performance of an eighteen months old girl at breakfast time: 'Bun. Butter. Jelly. Cakie. Jam. Cup of tea. Milkie.' To understand its significance we must imagine the game being played in the middle of a great sea of the un-named and hence (with some exceptions) the unfamiliar, the as yet undifferentiated. After the speaking of names has conferred a new status upon what was already familiar by use, the learning of new words adds fresh conquests—fresh objects are 'possessed' as they are differentiated. Then as further instances crop up and naming occasions are reduplicated, the word becomes a means of building up a category. ('Shoe. Another shoe. Two shoes.'—again at eighteen months.)

The second stage is reached when naming has progressed so far from touching that words begin to be used about things not present, and about events not actually taking place; and when words, in this way, come to be used *in place of things* they take on a much more powerful role. The naming game, in fact, represents a process of 'bringing into existence' the objects of the immediate environment, the here-and-now. But when the second stage is reached, the objects that *have been* named, but are no longer present, are brought in to assist in classifying what is present and relating it to the familiar. (On first meeting strawberries at two and a half: 'They are like cherries'—and, tasting them, 'They're just like sweeties'—and, finally, 'They are like ladybirds'.) What is being called into existence at this stage is an abiding world, a world that stays there when we move away or go to sleep—a world that provides prospect and retrospect as well as a here-and-now.

There is a paradox at the heart of all this. The words are old: they constitute a language that served the child's grandfathers and great-grandfathers before him. But every occasion for speaking them is a fresh one: in use, whether by child or grandfather they are on all but the most routine occasions not indeed newly minted, but newly meant. And the paradox is at its sharpest with the infant for whom there is no back-log of experience of what the words may in speaking be used to do.

Thus it is that in young children's efforts we recognize more clearly the nature of the process: how speech is generated not only to suit the situation—each new situation as it arises—but also to influence it in accordance with the speaker's needs and purposes. In other words he speaks to do more than meet the demands of the situation upon him—he speaks to *make something of it* for himself. What he makes of it, the direction of his curiosity, the tenor of his interpretation, the tentative constructions he places upon events—these in the course of his speaking reveal something of the sort of person he is becoming. He declares his individuality. And by a gradual process over a period of years he discovers his own individuality reflected in the responses other people make to his declarations.

To put the matter directly, all this amounts to saying that in speaking we represent the world to ourselves, and ourselves to other people. 'To represent' here means to 'make a representation', in the sense that we make a representation of a chair when we draw a chair, or a representation of the neighbourhood when we draw a map; in this sense also, that when we catch sight of a familiar face, what we have seen has matched something that we must have carried with us from previous seeing, a 'representation' of a face: and when our ears catch a familiar tune, the sound that has just been made must chime with an inner 'representation' of a sound we had heard on some previous occasion.

Language then is one way of representing experience, and before we can appreciate its particular role we must look at the importance of the process of representation itself. Learning in its broadest sense might be described as turning the unfamiliar into the familiar—not in a random way as my last examples might suggest (the chance heard tune, for instance) but in such a way as to relate one familiar item of experience with another. I knew a dog who grew very excited if he found a member of the household sticking stamps on to a letter: not only was the process familiar to him from past experience but it had been related, by experience, with another familiar event—being taken for a walk, and of course it was the anticipation of this that excited him.

Whatever might be said about dogs, it has been claimed that human beings internalize their experience of the world in the form of a *representation* of the world: and that whereas the lower animals respond directly to the stimulus of the actual environment, human beings react not directly but *via* this representation. The fruits of our past experience of the world are there in a coherent or organized form to assist our interpretation of what confronts us at a particular moment of time, the present. As I stick the stamps on a letter I too may anticipate the walk to the post-box, but I am likely to have in addition a far more complex and far-reaching set of anticipations taking into account such things as the appearance and personality and situation of the person I am writing to, and the probable outcomes of the news I have communicated. Moreover I can choose at any moment to think of that person, to recall his circumstances, to clarify my anticipations of his likely responses: it seems very unlikely that the dog can do anything at all like thinking quietly to himself 'It would be nice if someone were to write a letter and take me to the post'—he requires rather something in the present environment to set off the chain of expectation.

A representation lasts in time in a way that events themselves do not. One consequence of this we have seen—that we store experiences (to put it crudely): there are two other important consequences. First, we may work upon the representation: given the fact that our picture of what the world is like is subject to modification —as well as extension—by every new experience, we add now the notion that we may deliberately go back over experiences in order to make sense of them. That is to say, we work upon the representation to make it more orderly, more coherent. Secondly, a matter of the greatest importance, other people may work upon it too. The small boy who tells his mother what has been happening to him at school, goes back over the experiences, works upon the representation: but the representation is also very much affected by what she says in response. Thus, though each of us builds his own representation, what is built is in very large measure the picture of a world in common. We become experienced people in the light of other people's experiences as well as our own: the unfamiliar becomes familiar to us by virtue in part of our confidence in what other people have heard and seen and done.

We build in large measure a common world, a world in which we live together: yet each of us builds in his own way. My representation differs from yours not only because the world has treated us differently but also because *my way of representing* what happens to both of us will differ from yours. We are neither of us cameras. Admittedly, we construct a representation of the world we both inhabit: on your screen and mine, as on the sensitive plate in the camera, is reflected that world. But we are at the same time projecting on to the screen our own needs and desires. In this sense then, we build what is for each of us a representation of the world and at the same time is to each other a representation of a different individuality, another 'self'. More literally, it is by knowing in what terms I think of and respond to the objects and people and events of my environment that you know what sort of a person I am.

We interpret the present instant in order to turn what it offers us to our own advantage: that is to say we 'make something of' the situation (in one sense) in order to 'make something of' it in another sense. Past, present and future are interwoven here: we interpret the present by referring it to our representation of the world as we have experienced it, by bringing, in other words, the past to bear on it. Our purpose in doing so is to choose the appropriate response: in other words, to anticipate future events. Let me only add that as more and more of the world becomes familiar to us, the context into which we fit new experiences, by which we 'place' and interpret new experiences, becomes more complete and more effective as a basis for our predictions. Contrast the two-and-a-half-year-old confronting her first strawberries with the botanist identifying a rare plant.

Language is only one way of representing experience,

but as such it plays a key role because it becomes the means of organizing all the other forms of representation. It is for this reason that it has already found its way into our discussion of the representation-making process. First, it is as we have seen a way of classifying. The naming and touching game shows words in the closest possible relation with the use of the senses. To take one example of the importance of this, what is potentially a vast number of different colour sensations must be grouped under the word 'red' and this group related to other potentially vast groups under the words 'blue', 'green' and so on, before a child's colour experiences can enter significantly into his expectations about the world. In all his activities, words become the filing pins upon which successive encounters with objects and events are filed. (We must add a reminder that the language-using-cum-exploratory activities interact to feed each other at all points: that a child is stimulated to activity by the enticements of the world to his senses: and therefore that an environment rich in such enticements plays an essential part in the growth of his powers.)

Secondly, by reason of its own complex internal organization language can be used to impose, as it were, a grid upon the multiplicity of sense impressions. Built into language are relations of likeness, of oppositeness, of sequence, of hierarchy, of consequence; and as a child learns to operate the language systems he applies these relations to reduce to order the multiplicity of things in the world. He does not merely imitate sounds and so arrive at speaking; he learns to operate a system. Thus, at first 'flower' may be simply another name for 'daisy' and 'animal' another name for 'dog' but in due course he discovers he can use 'flower' to say things about buttercups and daisies and an immense number of other such objects. (And also that there is no satisfactory answer to the question 'What kind of a tail has a dog?' for the same sort of reason that he would not even ask 'What sort of a tail has an animal?') At a later stage he discovers that what seems *wide* on one occasion may seem *narrow* on another, and then he can begin to make sense of the fact that even the very, very narrow thing has width, just as the lowest things have *height*, and the lightest things *weight*: and that he can sensibly ask 'How heavy is your bag?' when it looks very light and 'How old is the kitten?' when it must be very young. In other words, he finds (but not in so many words) that oppositeness is a relationship that language systematically caters for.

Let us, in the third place, observe the fact that we habitually use language as a way of going back over experience, a way of *working upon* our representation of events. If we brood over something that has happened, our thinking has some of the characteristics of an inner dialogue and certainly it will take the form it does as a result of our past experiences of talking. (As Charles Morris explains it, we may not be using language symbols, but we shall certainly be using 'post-language symbols'.) But very frequently we in fact engage in talk as a means of going back over events: nothing is more familiar than the kind of gossip that goes on among participants after the 'big event'—the play, the party, the open day, the match, the wedding. There may well have been plenty of talk while they were still participating: but this is a different kind of talk because, no longer participants, they are in the role of spectators. Participants respond to ongoing events—they are 'responsible': spectators have no such responsibility, but are free to *savour* the past events in a quite different way. They will enjoy the behaviour of their party guests, for example, in a way that they could not while the guests were still behaving. They will savour and enjoy even the hardships and anxieties of the match—or 'the march'—in a way that they certainly did not enjoy them at the time.

The distinction between participants and spectators very roughly corresponds to a distinction linguists have made between two uses of speech. In the first, the participant form, speech and action are so closely complementary as to be often interchangeable. Interaction between two people—in a shop, for example—may be thought of as a chain of items any one of which may be speech, or action, or speech with action. The shopkeeper may say, 'Can I help you?' or he may merely stand opposite you in an expectant way: you may say, 'I'll take this, please' or pick up a bar of chocolate and give him the money. If you ask him, 'Have you a half-pound block?' he may say 'I'm sorry I haven't' or he may say 'Yes' and hand you one, or he may simply hand you one. Again, looking at another example in a slightly different way, if you have a bulky parcel to take through the door, you may manipulate the door somehow yourself, or you may use speech as a way of keeping the door open—by somebody else's agency.

You may agree that even in the simple examples given, speech may be seen to be used to organize our behaviour, to regulate both our individual and our co-operative activities. It would be more fully so, of course, when a group of people were engaged on a complicated joint enterprise. Such use of language by participants consti- tutes one way in which we construct a representation of experience and continue to adjust it—in our stride—as we come across the unexpected. Edward Sapir has sug- gested that it is from such uses 'in constant association with the colour and the requirements of actual contexts' that language acquires its 'almost unique position of intimacy' with human behaviour in general.

In the second of these two uses of speech, that corre- sponding to the role of spectator, language is used to refer to, report upon, and interpret action, rather than in substitution for it. Freed from the responsibility for action and interaction, we speak above all in order to shape experience, to interpret it—to work upon our representa- tion of the world. I want to distinguish three ways in which we may do this—though in doing so I must observe that in any one conversation it is likely that all three ways will be used to some degree. If I go back as a spectator over my own past experiences in conversation with you, then you are also in the role of spectator. It may well be that my incentive for doing so at all is to share these experiences with you, to savour them, enjoy them with you: at the same time I am shaping and inter- preting them and your comments will be helping me to do so. But the experiences I relate will sometimes be ones in which what happened was too unlike what I anticipated for me to adjust my world view, my body of expectations, while I was participating in them. In this case there is a positive *need* for me to go back and adjust, to 'come to terms' with the past events; and while in such situations you as a listener may sometimes be no more than a sounding board, you may of course sometimes be the major influence in bringing about the adjustment required. That is the first way of using conversation in the role of spectator: the events are those of my own experience and I shape them in order to share them. The second use could be illustrated from the same situation, seeing it from your point of view: let us, in all modesty, turn it round. Suppose as our conversation continues, you take up the role of spectator of your experiences and invite me to do the same. I am still engaged upon the shape of the world as I know it, but as I respond to you I shall be extending my picture to include in it some things that I have not experienced but you have. Of course, I cannot take over your experiences as though they were my own: inevitably it is still my own experience that I am working on: as I listen to your story I recombine elements of my own past experiences into new structures that correspond to the shape of your experiences. My representation is extended by this multiplication of its forms. My ability to anticipate events rests in this way partly upon the shape that experience has taken for other people.

Both these uses might have been regarded as ways of *improvising* upon my representation of the world: however the word applies more obviously to the third category of use. When in conversation we talk not about what has happened but what might happen, we open the way for a whole range of activities. I may speculate about what may happen to me with a close eye on actual possibilities —as might be the case if we were planning a joint undertaking. But in day dreaming the relation between what is imagined and what is likely to happen may be a very remote one: and of course we do carry on conversations which are a sociable form of day dreaming. The 'might-be' and the 'might-have-been' are pleasant topics of conversation and cover a whole range from sober, fairly realistic wish formulations to the extravagant fantasies of a Walter Mitty or a Billy Liar. Though the pleasure of improvising in this way upon our world representation may lie in the abandonment of any concern for the relation to reality and so for the predictive value, I would still see in such improvisations (in a world in which the strangest things sometimes happen) some connection with our urge to anticipate events or create the fullest context for whatever may occur. I see them, then, as a kind of testing out to the limits the possibilities of experience.

It should be added here that, if we accept as a rough definition of 'literature', 'the written language in the role of spectator', the literature we write may fall into any of the three categories we have considered and the literature we read may fall into the second or the third.

Thus, while it is true that we use language to shape experiences even as we participate in them, the shaping more typically takes place as we go back over experience in the role of spectators. Freed from practical responsibility, we are able to *savour* the feelings that accompanied events rather than act upon them, attend to the pattern of actions and circumstances, evaluate against a broader framework than we were able to apply in the course of the actual experience. Do we *give* this shape, or do we *find* it? The question must remain an open one: it seems probable that the structure of our world-picture reflects both order in the universe and our own particular way of *representing* the world—the shaping force of our own inner needs and desires.

To speak of language in the role of participant and in the role of spectator is to make a broad division in terms of the relation between the speaker and the situation. I want now to look more closely at language itself and suggest a three-fold division.

A great deal of talk is of the kind that Sapir called 'expressive'. It tends to tell us as much about the speaker as it does about the subjects of his talk. It is speech that follows the contours of the speaker's consciousness, a kind of verbalizing of the self. Often it will be intelligible only to someone who knows almost as much about the situation of the speaker as he does himself. Sapir suggests that as expressive speech sheds its more personal, unique, individual, subjective features and refers more explicitly to the actual world, it turns into 'referential' speech—the speech by which we participate in the world's affairs—informing people, explaining things, arguing, persuading, asking questions and so on. I want to add another 'wing' to Sapir's diagram; if expressive speech remains in the centre—a matrix, speech not subjected to the kind of pressure that makes it referential—then I should put referential (or transactional) speech on the one side, and 'poetic' or 'formal' speech on the other. This is also arrived at by subjecting expressive speech to particular demands, but they are demands of a different kind. They concern the *formal* characteristics of the utterance, and in particular its coherence, unity, wholeness. As speech, it is rare; the nearest examples will be occasional utterances in the course of successful dramatic improvisations: and this may serve to suggest the nature of the demands I have referred to—they are the kind of demands any artist makes upon himself in order to produce an object, a work of art.

Writing is of course rooted in speaking, though the two processes are very different. Because writing is *premeditated* utterance, because there is a time gap between its utterance and its reception, the shaping process I have been writing about may be fuller or deeper or sharper in its effect than it normally is in speech.

It seems probable that children's first attempts at writing will naturally rely heavily upon their speech experience, and will be of a kind we should classify as expressive: and that with more experience we shall find it differentiating in the two directions, both towards the referential and towards the poetic. Let me in conclusion suggest that the following extracts indicate better than I could explain the transitional categories that very much good writing in the Primary School will fall into. The first is by a ten-year-old boy: the practical task in hand has shaped his writing in the direction of the referential:

How I Filtered my Water Specimens

When we were down at Mr. Harris's farm I

brought some water from the brook back with
me. I took some from a shallow place by the oak
tree, and some from a deep place by the walnut
tree. I got the specimens by placing a jar in the
brook and let the water run into it. Then I
brought them back to school to filter.... The
experiment that I did shows that where the water
was deeper and was not running fast there was
a lot more silt suspended as little particles in
the water. You could see this by looking at the
filter paper, where the water was shallow and fast
there was less dirt suspended in it.

There are, as you see, expressive features interwoven
with the referential: it *was* an oak tree, and it *was* a
walnut tree—he knows because he was there—for him
this was a part of what happened but they are features
of his landscape rather than features of the experiment
he sets out to describe.

The next example I can only leave with you. It is a
catalogue by a seven-year-old girl—a kind of writing we
are familiar with. But in this case I believe the rhythms
she set up in the writing began to exercise some control
over what she wrote: the writing, I suggest, moves
towards the artistic, towards the language of poetry.

Class I had Monday off and Tuesday off and all
the other classes had Monday and Tuesday off
and we played hide-and-seek and my big sister hid
her eyes and counted up to ten and me and my
brother had to hide and I went behind the Dust-bin
and I was thinking about the summer and the
butter-cups and Daisies all those things and fresh
grass and violets and roses and lavender and the
twinkling sea and the star in the night and the
black sky and the moon.

Bibliography

Chukovsky, K., *From Two to Five* (translated by Miriam Morton), (University of California Press, 1963)

Harding, D. W., 'The Role of the Onlooker', in *Scrutiny*, Vol. VI, No. 3 (1937)

Langer, Susanne K., *Philosophical Sketches*, (Johns Hopkins Press, 1962)

Luria, A. R. & Yudovich, F. Ia., *Speech and the Development of Mental Processes in the Child* (translated by J. Simon), (Staples Press, 1959)

Piaget, Jean, *Six Psychological Studies* (translated by Anita Tenzer), (Random House, 1968)

Piaget, Jean, *Play, Dreams and Imitation in Childhood* (translated by C. Gattegno and F. H. Hodgson), (Heinemann, 1951)

Sapir, Edward, *Culture, Language and Personality*, (University of California Press, 1961)

Vygotsky, L. S., *Thought and Language* (translated by E. Hanfmann and G. Vakar), (M.I.T. Press, 1962)

||||||||||||||||||||||||||||||||||||||||||||||||||||||||||||||||||||||||||||||||||||||||||||||||||||||||

In the following account of '*how* children achieve the phenomenon of language...', Winifred Fawcus complements the last article. She extends the stress Professor Britton lays on the social factors that affect language development. Like other writers in the book, she produces examples which illustrate aspects of Professor Britton's models: for instance, there are pieces of spontaneous speech that are moving towards the 'poetic' mode of utterance.

||||||||||||||||||||||||||||||||||||||||||||||||||||||||||||||||||||||||||||||||||||||||||||||||||||||||

EXPERIENCE AND THE LANGUAGE TO POSSESS IT

Winifred Fawcus

Without systematic teaching as the school knows it, many children beginning school arrive talking effectively, already masters to some degree of the processes of 'being and possessing' described in the previous paper. The following snatches of talk were from children who had just come into a reception class in an economically deprived area of a north-eastern town.

A boy on his first day at school offered 'I call me Mark Hamilton' as the first move in an introduction to his headmistress. A girl requested her teacher to 'Write here are Mammy, Garry, Karin in the park' while another at her shoulder remarked, 'Mammy, Garry, Karin—that's yourself'. A child sweeping the classroom was heard to say 'This is breaking my back' and later in the home corner 'You'll eat this biscuit if you like it or not' and 'Come on, out! out!' Throughout those early school days came numerous examples of variety of language usage, range of vocabulary, sentence pattern and intonation. Even when hold over grammatical form seemed less secure, examples showed how mistakes could be seen as the result of language knowledge rather than language ignorance. A girl helping the headmistress to fill a tin with bobbins announced 'I've fulled them'. Another, witness to a minor accident, said 'She's fellen down'. A boy informed his teacher 'He brung a car'. The teacher in the reception class expects to be able to talk with, talk to, and be understood by the majority of her five-year-old charges. Only a minority tend to be thought of as problem cases.

The snippets of talk reported above might well serve to illustrate the language gains that Professor Britton's article deals with. The concern in this article is with *how* children achieve the phenomenon of langauge, *how* children exploit to the full situations that promote language development. Certain factors are well established. Speech apparatus is there in all of us. Listening organs develop very early in a child's life. If hearing is healthy very young babies respond to noise and infants discover that they too can make sounds when they babble. Most infants play with sounds and practice them, especially it seems, those that give most pleasure. It is human to be born into a talking society and the sounds of people talking must drift in and out of consciousness as do sights and surfaces and other perceptible characteristics. Although the ability to make and to hear sounds is innate, sounds that are made and heard as words belong to the environment. Language reflects the total life of a community in which a child is reared and in Harold Ruggs' terms (*Imagination*, published posthumously 1963, Harper & Row) embraces all that is 'done, made, aimed at, thought, believed, feared and desired by the people talking', in addition to all the things and events surrounding them which they talk about. The young human could not grow as a person without identifying himself with his immediate community. He learns to be a speaker because it's largely through the spoken word that the environment, including its behaviour and his own as part of it, becomes established for him. He discovers, too, albeit unconsciously, that as a speaker he can more readily secure his position in the family circle and make language act for him as it does for the other members.

Fortunately, most parents bend over backwards to increase a child's incentives to utter and to listen. Encouraged by the response to his own efforts, warmed and relaxed by affection, he becomes interested in the speech of others. With encouragement flows the energy to assimilate, imitate and finally to adapt what he has heard for his own verbal behaviour. A communicating child is one many parents have looked forward to since that day they mistakenly identified a babbled 'ma-ma' or 'pa-pa' to indicate themselves.

Anthology after anthology of transcripts of tapes of parents and children talking might be compiled with infinite patience and still not cover the extent of the contribution of the adult to the child's command of language. Esther Milner, investigating the relationship between reading readiness and patterns of parent-child interaction,

42

in 1951, found that for six year olds, the habit of talking and eating with parents at meal-times was top of her list of factors influencing the readiness of the top-scorers. The 'touching and naming' example in the previous paper came from an eighteen-month-old girl at the breakfast table. Recently Professor Basil Bernstein has shown how close is the relationship of general talking between parents and children at home and mental capacity to learn in school. The following extract of a conversation between a father and his three-year-old daughter Diana about a television programme seen by both the day before illustrates some of the gains of a few minutes talking together.

D. A penguin came out of the water and
F. Yes.
D. And the fence knocked down.
F. Who knocked the fence down?
D. The walrus.
F. It wasn't the walrus. It was Pulgit...
D. Panda!
F. No.
D. Pulgit—What? Pul ... git ... the bison!
F. The bison. That's right.
D. Pulgit the bison is a very good name ... Pulgit.
F. Yes.
D. Do you like Pulgit name ... for a bison?
F. Yes.
D. I Pul ... *my* Bison is called Pulgit, too!
F. Oh, you're calling him Pulgit, are you?
D. My bison's called Pulgit, Mummy.
M. Pulgate? ... erm!
D. Pulgit. And—knocked my door down.
F. Did he?
D. It was on ... and he knocked my window down. I mean, on my pigsty and he couldn't 'cos it was too hard.
F. Oh!
D. He nearly did!! He—just a half-off. Just a tiny hole ... but the big bad, the big pig hadn't central heating put in and the little pigs didn't like it at all.

The father is seen as listener, encourager, responder and helper. The child recalls with his help words to fix what was seen yesterday. She sorts out and does some simple ordering. She savours new ideas now more firmly grasped and immediately applies 'a very good name' to something of her own. There follows an illustration of the young child's practical imagination creating a new idea.

Children who have frequent experience of parents or other adults who will talk with them in relaxed and companionable ways are well prepared to use talking as an integral part of any activity, whether or not an adult is participating. Vygotsky maintained that social speech precedes ego-centric speech and in the monologue that follows one can imagine how much the child has taken to himself, adapting patterns and words that have often been said to him. He uses them in his own way as an indivisible part of his play with bricks. He too is a three-year-old. His father who recorded the tape reports that the mother was in the room and that although appearing to inform her, he did not place himself within her view, nor did he turn round to see if she was watching. He did not appear to expect any response.

> I am going to make something
> I am going to make a chimney Mummy
> I am going to make a door well
> Mummy, I have finished, make a fire when I have
>   finished
> Where's that one? Always falling. Threw it down
>   Mummy.
> What I make with the Lego Mummy?
> I make a table ... The Vicar ... Steps to climb
>   and read
> I make a big one
> I want to make it bigger
> That bigger
> That very big one—make another one on top
> I make another one just now
> I want the steps
> Are you watching Mummy?
> I make steps Mummy on there

I am going to make a piano as well
This going to stand ladder up same as that
Mum just doing that

———————

All knocked down
Don't worry

Words can be seen to reinforce the play and the play to stimulate the language. Interesting concepts are emerging with the activity—'make a door well' 'big' 'bigger' and 'very big'. There is evidence of planning—'something' becomes several items named before they are made. At the end of the cascade comes the direct echo of his mother's reassuring 'Don't worry'.

If a child has nobody but adults to talk with, he may arrive at school with no practice in understanding or talking with children he will meet in the classroom. A head teacher reports of one such child, 'This small child with her adult language even to intonation and expression, is cut off from other children because of her adult conversation. They do not understand her and cannot communicate with her. Because she is so used to talking to adults she cannot be bothered with trying to find the key to their language and so there is very little, if any, communication. This has caused her to withdraw—and she is not a particularly happy child.' The three-year-old of the Lego monologue, referred to below as D, is talking with his nine-year-old sister H.C. while both are cutting newspapers to make patterns.

H.C. Now look, put the paper away, we are going to tidy up.
D. I am going to tidy up. I have finished H.C.
H.C. This is going to be a good one
D. What that? What is it? Can I have a look? Hey that good. A different one now like that. You make a mess.
H.C. Now let me see what this one looks like.
D. What is it? You mustn't make a mess like that 'cos Miss Marshall coming. Have you finished H.C.? What doing with that H.C.?
H.C. This makes it nicer.

D.   Can I have that one? That is the last one 'cos
we do some morrow. What that about?

H.C. It is a little one.

D.   Just the last one. Can I have a look. Put it like
that. There now. I got a lot there. I got a very
big one there.

H.C. Come on, put these away.

D.   We finished. 'Cos we are.

H.C., like many children of her age, is absorbed in the
activity even though it is she who introduces the idea
of tidying up, and she makes the briefest response to D's
chatty questioning. But the brother and sister relationship
allows D at times to verbally assert himself and his
language enables him to reinforce his position with his
own logic ' 'Cos Miss Marshall coming', ' 'Cos we do
some morrow'. It deserts him at the end—'We finished.
'Cos we are'.

The adult close to the young child has a stake in his
language development. Other children, for most of the
time they are together, are far more likely to be concerned
with getting satisfaction from the activity of the moment
and any one child may be seen as companion sharing the
interest, a prop for the play, or a nuisance. The language
of child companionship, acceptance and disapproval
helps children to discover themselves as other children
find them. Such language is necessary for the making
and reshaping of relationships so that children may learn
from each other.

All children and no adults to speak with can be as
limiting as all adults and no children, especially when a
child is a regular member of a group none of whom has
had much enrichment from the language of adults. There
have been several studies of twins and of young institu-
tionalized children, notably those of Luria and Kellmer
Pringle, to show the extent of this impoverishment.

Another kind of handicap faces the child whose parents
and companions use exclusively what Bernstein calls
'restricted codes' of language. Inside the family society
these forms will provide an appropriate instrument for
living together. They may often provide a child with

rugged and colourful expression. It is when he moves outside the group, to school for instance, that his exclusive use of a restricted code may mark him off as linguistically deprived on at least three counts. One, his language differs from 'standard' English; two, it has not encouraged him to explore his environment with anything like the verbal detail and variety that more 'elaborated' code users achieve; and three, his more limited language acts as a barrier to easy communication with his teacher who uses language for purposes and in ways strange to him. He has less to say to others, and fewer verbal forms to say it with. He cannot be known and he cannot know to the same degree.

To be known and to know is another way of saying 'we represent the world to ourselves and ourselves to other people'! Somehow, through infancy, persons to talk with and the things that are and the events that happen are intricately woven to equip young children to 'make a representation' in Professor Britton's terms. The more things there are to name, the more filing pins are needed; but with the help of words a sense of the relationships between things gradually replaces the sense of their separateness. Professor Britton has illustrated the process whereby 'flower' and 'animal' come to be accepted as categories and as such can be used to refer respectively to any flower or animal.

A three-year-old sang:

> I'm thinking about things
> Thinking about big liners
> The weight of them
> And very big trees
> The thickness of them
> The wideness of the thickness

He did not read before his schooldays. Words used here were heard. He tells more of things than their names and is thinking about qualities he's attaching to them. This song and the next one come from *Songs and Pictures by a Child* compiled by his mother under a pseudonym in 1936 and now out of print.

Chestnuts, floating down the river
Floating, floating, floating,
Down river under the bridge.
Chestnuts floating down the river
Acorns not floating very much,
Only a little bit.
How nicely they grow,
Sometimes big, sometimes small,
Sometimes medium sized
How nicely they grow
All horse chestnuts still floating about,
Up and down rivers
Up and down sea,
Up and down rivers
Up and down sea.

Words are not just names, they represent the capture and hoarding of sensory impressions that flood us daily enabling us to know more about the things named and ourselves naming them. Both songs are examples of 'expressive' speech in the terms of Sapir's definition referred to by Professor Britton. Sapir describes the movement from the purely 'expressive' to the 'referential'. These songs which possess qualities of 'coherence, unity and wholeness' fall more readily into Professor Britton's second 'wing', the poetic. It seems that progress towards either 'wing', the 'referential' or the 'poetic', will depend upon a child's growing awareness that just as things can be talked about, so too can feelings and perceptions aroused in connection with the things. Giving honest answers to his questions is one means of helping him express his fuller experience of the thing. He can docket answers for future reference and understanding of new things. The categorizing process mentioned earlier allows him freedom to make his own discoveries about the relationships, for instance, between floating chestnuts and floating acorns, the weight of big liners and the thickness of big trees.

We can add considerably to a child's general store by sharing with him the experience of others through picture and story book, nursery rhyme and poem. I knew the father of the child whose songs are quoted and realized how much the child's awareness of the quality of things was stimulated by stories, poems and pictures shared with him.

Two different kinds of response are illustrated in the next two examples. They are taped from a girl aged five who 'read' to a teddy bear. The first was stimulated by C. Patti's 'The Happy Owls' read to her some weeks previously. The book is forcefully illustrated.

> The owl is awake at night
> The wise wise white wise owl
> The wise owl is asleep at night
> In the morning
> In the daytime
> He is awake
> At night
> When he squalls his squalling song
> Have you ever heard him?

The recorder notes 'Nothing of the narrative is mentioned, though this is not surprising as the story content itself was rather uninteresting ... the story, and the fact that there were two owls, has gone. It is the owl as a bird with which she is concerned, and it is her relationship to the owl that she is establishing ... It is to be noticed that no visual account is given. Her impression is felt, haptic*, not visually recorded. This is a purely connotative meaning which could hardly be revealed by direct questioning. Allison's poems generally make less demands on her vocabulary than her stories, yet they are much more intense, colourful and meaningful.'

The second happened as the child flicked over the pages of a book picked up at random.

> I think I will just / now Teddy you had better
> listen because I am going to tell you some poems /
> poetries today / 'cos / because I have forgotten

---

* A term used by Ludwig Müenz and Viktor Löwenfeld (*Plastiche Arbeiten Blinder* (Bruenn, 1934)) and by Herbert Read (*Education through Art* (Faber)). As opposed to the 'visual' type, the haptic is concerned with 'projecting his inner world into the picture' ... the haptic type attempts to 'create a synthesis between his tactile perceptions of external reality, and his own subjective experiences'.

this little story / it's a nice little story but I have
forgotten it / so / so I will sing the poems about it /.

Here is a little cat
Her fur is smooth as mink
The mink that the coat is
Is absolutely beautiful
But how could she get a little pink bow?
I'll ask her mistress
That's it.
She met a little mouse
She met a little mouse
She met a little mouse
How do you do little mouse?
Won't you come in, little mouse?
In my playroom?
And well and well and well
Little mouse said
Oh yes! Oh yes! Oh yes!
She met a little mouse
And she killed it and ate it
And she ate it up.
And that was the end of the little mouse.
Now wasn't that nice teddy?
Cheep cheep cheep cheep cheep.

The recorder adds 'Allison says about the book—"This
is a nice little story, but I have forgotten it". In fact she
has never heard it. What she meant was that it looked as
if it could have been an interesting story, but as she did
not know it, she wasn't going to be bothered to construct
one at the moment.' With stories and poems and her
previous experience to draw upon she talks her own
stories or 'poems' to complement the pictures.

In the introduction to *Songs and Pictures* the com-
piler writes: 'The examples shown here illustrate his
(her son's) very free expression of the feelings aroused
by the things he has seen or heard, and may be accepted
as a child's first attempts at self-expression as a natural
activity before being subjected to a systematized and
formal education.' True, 'formal' here must be read in the
context of 1936 educational practice, but does something
different have to happen to encourage language develop-

ment in institutions specially designed to educate? If 'teacher' can be substituted for 'English teacher,' Frank Whitehead puts the 'how' of home and the 'how' of school language mastery into perspective: 'The main business of the English teacher is not instruction in any direct sense, not even teaching in the sense which may be applicable in some other subjects. It is the provision of abundant opportunity to use English under the conditions which will most conduce to improvement: opportunity, that is, to use his mother-tongue in each of its four modes (listening, speaking, reading and writing) and for all the varied purposes (practical, social, imaginative, creative) which make up its totality; opportunity moreover to use it under expert guidance and in situations which will develop ultimately his power to be self-critical about his own efforts.' Perhaps too all teachers need to forget from time to time their teaching role in the classroom, to be instead spontaneous sharers in excitement and experience and the adventure of learning. A teacher of young children especially needs to respect the inner fantasy and outer play as well as the more concrete terms of reference by which children create a reality for themselves. Above all teachers need to recognize the language stepping stones for individual charges in their temporary care.

A child entered a remedial group and on her first day there, volunteered in a game of 'What am I?'

I is skinny, What is I? (A worm)

Five months later she was offering

I am small
I have brown hair
I have blue eyes
I wear a dress
I can bite and scratch
Sometimes I am vicious (my baby sister).

In that short period some of her language problems had been identified and provided for by a caring adult who happened to be her teacher. The process was a subtle one and would defy precise analysis, but it resembled in many ways what would naturally go on in a family where parents enjoyed putting a child in the way of experience and the language to possess it.

Acknowledgements

I am grateful to the following for the loan of recordings of children talking and for the use of their notes made at the time: Mary Lowes, Lil Thompson, Arnold Pattinson, Nicholas Jennings.

Bibliography

Bernstein, Basil, 'Social Class and Linguistic Development. A Theory of Social Learning' in Halsey, Floud & Anderson (eds.) *Education, Economics and Society*, (N.Y. Free Press, 1961)

Bland, Doreen (arranged by), *Songs and Pictures by a Child*, (Williams and Norgate, 1936)

De Cecco, John P., *The Psychology of Language, Thought and Instruction*, (Holt, Rinehart and Winston, 1967)

Lewis, M. M., *Language, Thought and Personality in Infancy and Childhood*, (Harrap, 1963)

Lewis, M. M., *Language and the Child*, (N.F.E.R., 1969)

Luria, A. R. & Ludovitch, I., *Speech and Development of Mental Processes in the Child*, (Staple Press, 1959)

Milner, E., 'A Study of the Relationship between Reading-readiness in Grade 1 Schoolchildren and Patterns of Parent-Child Interaction' in *Child Development*, 22

Müenz, Ludwig & Löwenfeld, Viktor, *Plastiche Arbeiten Blinder*, (Bruenn, 1934)

Pringle, M. L. K., 'The Effects of Early Deprivation on Speech Development. A comparative study of four year olds in a nursery school and in residential nurseries' in *Language and Speech*, Oct.-Dec. 1958

Read, Herbert, *Education through Art*, (Faber, 1943)

Vygotsky, L. S., *Thought and Language*, (M.I.T. Press, 1962)

Whitehead, Frank, *The Disappearing Dais*, (Chatto and Windus, 1966)

We might say a great many complicated and subtle things about the value of creative writing and literature in school. But unless we see them as both rooted in commonplace habits of ordinary speech we shall not understand them aright or use them as effectively as we could.

This quotation is from an essay by James Britton about the teaching of literature (in which, incidentally, he first developed his spectator/participant distinction).* In another book edited by Professor Britton, *Talking and Writing* (Methuen), this subject is explored suggestively from a number of points of view (the book also includes an introductory note on the socio-linguistic work of Basil Bernstein by Dennis Lawton,† and a very useful bibliography).

In the last two decades, such writers as Marjorie Hourd, David Holbrook and Sybil Marshall‡ have demonstrated again and again what is suppressed in children if their teachers concentrate on the mechanics, the rules, of writing. They have attacked the crassness represented classically in the case cited by John Blackie in *Good Enough for the Children* (Faber), which Brian Jackson uses for the epigraph of *English versus Examinations* (Chatto and Windus):

'My father is on the broad side and tall side. My

---

* In James Britton (ed.), *Studies in Education: The Arts and Current Tendencies in Education* (Evans Bros.).

† An introductory note by Professor Bernstein himself can be found in *Some Aspects of Oracy*, edited by Andrew Wilkinson (University of Birmingham). See also Professor Bernstein's 'A Critique of the Concept of "Compensatory Education"' in *Education for Democracy* edited by David Rubinstein and Colin Stoneman (Penguin); and Dennis Lawton, *Social Class, Language and Education* (Routledge).

‡ See, respectively: *The Education of the Poetic Spirit* (Heinemann) and (with G. E. Cooper) *Coming into Their Own* (Heinemann); *English for the Rejected* (C.U.P.); and *An Experiment in Education* (C.U.P.).

father was a hard working man and he had a
lot of money. He was not fat or thin.... His age
was about thirty years when he died, he had a
good reputation, he is a married man. When he was
in hospital I went to see him every Sunday
afternoon. I asked him how he was going on, he
told me he was getting a lot better. My father was
very kind to me and gave me and my cousins
cigarette cards. He likes doing woodwork, my
father, for me, and he likes a little game of cards
now and then; or a game of darts. He chops the
wood and saws the planks and he is a handsome
man but he is dead. He worked at the rubber
works before he died.'

9-year-old boy

Teacher's comment: 'Tenses. You keep mixing past
and present.'

With an increasing concern that teachers should
attempt to see and foster children's intellectual, emotional
and social development unfragmentedly, as a whole (see
John Dixon's *Growth through English*, (O.U.P.)), has
come a recognition by some teachers that such skills as
the ability to spell or to punctuate are best taught, for
the most part, incidentally; and that books full of mechanical exercises are worse than useless.* In *The Excitement of Writing* (edited by A. B. Clegg, (Chatto and
Windus)), many teachers testify to this. Moreover, Sir
Alec Clegg writes:

It is sometimes held that a pupil's ability to use
words well does not apply generally to all his work
and that if he writes poetry or expressive prose
really well it does not follow that he will be able

---

* 'Spelling Etc.' below (pages 153 to 174) offers an account of the
teaching of the conventions from this point of view. For a devastating
attack on the assumptions of an N.F.E.R. English Progress Test, see
David Holbrook, 'The Text-book Myth', Chapter 10 of *The Secret
Places* (Methuen). On the effects of examinations, see the 'Introduction' to Brian Jackson (ed.), *English versus Examinations* (Chatto &
Windus).

to give a clear account of a scientific experiment...
All the evidence which has been received from
the schools of the County at every stage from
the Infant school to the sixth form leads to the
belief that this contention is in the main false and
that the ability to use words well is an indivisible
achievement which once learned will be used
effectively in whatever kind of writing the child
does, though this does not of course alter the fact
that the boy's interests will lead him more in one
direction than in another. (page 5)

James Britton and Nancy Martin in the present book
(and Harold Rosen in *Talking and Writing**) can be seen
as moving on from this position. They explain and
develop it (at the same time as they qualify it to some
extent). Thus, in the following long examination of
children's writing, Miss Martin employs Professor
Britton's models to undermine old assumptions about
how to promote children's basic language skills: she
shows the extent to which children meaningfully engage
with, and represent, their world will depend on how
much opportunity they are given to write expressively;
and she demonstrates the *fundamental* importance of
imaginative work to the development of language
resources.

---

* Edited by James Britton (Methuen).

IIIIIIIIIIIIIIIIIIIIIIIIIIIIIIIIIIIIIIIIIIIIIIIIIIIIIIIIIIIIIIIIIIIIIIIIIIIIIIIIIIIIIIIIIIIIIIIIIIIIIIII

WHAT ARE THEY UP TO?

A study of a week's output in writing from three classes, one aged 7, one aged 11, and one aged 9

Nancy Martin

This study of all that the children wrote in a sample week is intended to document from actual examples some of the relationships between language and experience which James Britton explores in the second article in this book. In doing this I have attempted to apply some of the ways of looking at children's writing that we are using in the enquiry into the development of writing abilities at the secondary level which we are carrying out at the London Institute of Education under the sponsorship of the Schools Council.

I am going to look in some detail at what seem to be the functions of the different kinds of writing done by three classes in three different schools, one aged six to seven years, one aged nine to ten, and one aged ten to eleven. All the written work that each child did in one week was collected and read many times in an attempt to answer the question: 'What are these children using this language for?'

I have tried to answer this question in terms of the broad distinctions of language use that James Britton describes, so that when the terms 'expressive', 'referential', and 'poetic' are used, they will have the same meaning as he attaches to them.

I begin the story with the seven year olds at the stage when the children have internalized a good deal of the talk they have been sharing in for about five years, and are now able to engage in the dialogue in the head of which writing is a modified expression; that is, they 'speak' on paper at some length, without the physical stimulus of another person who keeps the talk going. It is true, of course, that they are writing for their teacher who will read what they have written and will 'reply' to it in some way, but she is not 'listening'—and participating—as they write. In their writings (as in their spoken utterances) they are discovering themselves, and discovering the world around them.

A. The seven-year-olds: a week's work

The school

The work came from a class of 24 children (unstreamed), 11 boys and 13 girls, mostly aged 7 (or nearly 7) in a County Infant School in a commuter area for Wolverhampton.

This written work represents only a proportion of all the things the children engaged in during the week under review; but it does represent *all the writing* they did.

The school has an informal organization with a varying pattern of self-chosen and teacher-directed work. Each day begins with news-writing (or telling) as they come in to school and settle down; parents can also come for this first half hour of the day, which is social, informal and rooted in talk.

This is followed by assembly with some music—again this is informal—the children sit on the floor in self-chosen groups and news is exchanged.

After this the children and their teachers pursue various activities as they wish; but the children's writings show that certain features in the week's work are constant. Though no two writing books are alike, some things have been done by all. Each child, for instance, has done some Mathematics; each child has done some Science: all begin the day with a diary entry; all have written at least one story ('My Story'). Besides these items, there are letters to their Headmistress, newspaper reports written by them, poems and a few informative pieces about objects, creatures or operations that have interested the writers, and very occasionally something informational such as an account of the Romans in Britain.

So the overall picture shows two areas of teacher-directed work that all write up in a similar way—mathematics and science—and outside these, any area of their experience may be written about. Some children who will have been spending more time on other activities do less writing than others, but the direction (with time allotted) towards diaries on the one hand and stories on the other means that every child uses his own language to make something of his outer and inner experiences for himself.

The children belong to the County Library and they may change their books every dinner hour. Furthermore there are books set about the school where they catch the eye. So the writing that appears in the children's books must be seen against a background of other people's writing (books) and much talk with each other and with adults (the children constantly go into the Headmistress's room, which is also the staff room, to talk to her, ask questions or look for their friends).

The writings

The average amount written by each member of the class was 20 full pages, excluding pictures, and this covered about 15 different items; 10 of the stories are between 4 and 10 pages in length. The writings reflect the children's lives at home and in school, their special interests (animals, football, birthdays, play, friendships, food, etc.), their fantasies, their relationships with teachers, families and friends, and also the work they had been doing in school.

Within the average of 15 different pieces of written work each child had made four or five diary entries and had written one or two generally long stories; he had also done two or more pieces of work headed 'Mathematics' and two or three brief reports of scientific experiments. Over and above this minimum most children had written a good many other things. The only direct copying from books that occurred in this sample was a brief item of 'National news' which about half the children added at the end of their diary entries; often this was copied verbatim but not always.

The referential and the poetic

The first thing one observed about the writing which all children did was that the language of the personal news and stories was sharply different from the language of the mathematics and science. James Britton suggests that children's early writing will rely heavily on their experi-

58

ence of speech and is likely to be of a kind that we should classify as expressive, and that, as they gain experience, we should expect to find it being modified in two directions, sometimes towards the referential and sometimes towards the poetic.

In these writings we found such differentiation; the personal news items are very like written down speech, and though often not overtly expressive, if by an act of imagination one re-sets these bald statements into their context of seven-year-old voices, gestures, hesitations and facial expressions, one can be in no doubt that these are personal declarations—as are all the items which are initiated by the children; the stories, however, in addition to being highly expressive have formal elements which mark them out as different from the news items. The science and mathematics are different in another way; they have been directed towards the referential and are not primarily expressive, though as we shall see, some of them contain expressive elements, and I am later going to suggest that the function of these expressive elements is to relate these outer discoveries to the writers' inner world-picture.

The diaries

'In written speech,' says Vygotsky, 'we create the situation and represent it to ourselves.' Here is what David wrote as his news item for May 5th:

> Today it's my birthday and I had a spiaragrath and a airfix Bumper Books and I played with my spiarograht and when Daddy brought me to school hes going back and his going to play with my spiarograth and today Gary is coming to tea and we will play subuiteo and football and with my spiarograth and we might have a game at table soccer and Gary will have to go at about 8 o'clock and I will go and help him cary his things then I will go home and go to bed.

He has re-created some of the events of the day by recalling them and framing them in words; furthermore he has created the shape of some future events as he expects they will happen. This diary item, and hundreds like it, is closely tied to the 'here and now' of actual events; it is a representation based on memory and experience and its order is the order in which events happen to us, one after the other; the bald statements in temporal order demand few other connectives than 'and' and 'then', and its only coherence lies in the fact that all the statements are so joined. It is essentially written down speech. David speaks on paper just as he would if he were giving an oral account of what he did yesterday, but under this apparent similarity lurks a tremendous intellectual and linguistic difference. It is an imagined and not a real conversation that is taking place; there is no actual listener as he writes, and his sense of an audience, or someone to communicate with, is secondary to the fact that he is above all making a representation of his experience to himself.

In speech the changing motives of the speakers determine at every moment the turns that it will take. It does not have to be consciously directed—the dynamic situation takes care of that. Writing, on the other hand, is detached from the actual situation and requires deliberate analytical action. The young writer at 7 years old has to be aware of the sound structure of each word and reproduce it in alphabetical symbols, and he has to be explicit in a way that he never has to be in speech. Above all he is without the stimulus of the actual situation and the speech of other people. Vygotsky observes that the motives for writing are often far from the child—are more intellectualized and further removed from actual needs. And think of the laboriousness of it! It is not, therefore, surprising that at seven, relatively little of their experience is verbalized in writing—David's diary items about his birthday, for example, carry little sense of how he felt about it; his feelings are not events and the familiar narrative form does not demand it. In speech his feelings would be expressed in tone of voice and movement and tempo and volume. The direct expression of self-awareness comes later; at seven, judging from the diaries, patterns of events would seem to be as much as the children can manage, though the stories suggest that here self-awareness is beginning to creep in.

Occasionally a more extended item appears—an anecdote for instance, and any such extension demands a correspondingly more complex language. Here is what Mary wrote:

> On Saturday morning I went down to the shops with mummy to get some stuff for the party when I was there I saw Mrs. Bowaller I took her to see Shandy who was in the car I told her that he was a hunting dog mr. Bowaller wanted to know what things he hunted and I said that he hunted anything and mr. Bowaller said I hope he dosnt hunt teachers I am off. But Andrew said that he didnt.

The greater explicitness of her re-creation of the shopping incident makes demands on her language of a different sort from David's bald items; e.g. '... I went down to the shops ... *when I was there* I saw Mrs. Bowaller I took her to see Shandy *who was in the car.*' Then she moves into reported speech and out of it into direct speech and ends with the statement 'But Andrew said that he didnt.'

The stories: moving towards the poetic

Here is another kind of representation: this one is not tied to the actual—to the way things *are*—but is a representation of the way the writer *feels* about things. Ian wrote:

> One day there lived a farmer he was very very rich and this farmer had a son and when the farmer died he gave the farm to his son and also gave his money to his son and his son felt very proud because he had the horses and the cows and the pigs and the cattle and sheep but the farmers son was not satisfied because he wanted some hens and a hen house built for him and one day he heard of

61

some men coming round building things for people and he said to himself I'll ask thees men to build me a hen house and buy some hens and be happy. and perhaps there wouldn't be any need to have anything else on the farm because the farm might be full of animals but if not he might buy some more sheep to put in the cattle shed some more pigs to put in the pig sty but if there is too much on the farm he would sell some and might be even richer then he would have much more money than he had last time and at this he was so happy that he danced all round the farm untill he was very very tired out and so he lay down and went to sleep and he dremt a dreem that he had never dremt befor and it was a very nice dream and he dremt that a fairy cam in the night and when he saw the fairy he couldn't beleave what he saw because by the fairy was a hen house and when he went by the hen house a flash of light came and the next thing he saw was some hens flying about and half of them coming out of the hen house to start flying. and some of them came with their mothers so there mothers could teach them to fly like other hens. and at there the farmers son whoke up and to his surprise there was a hen house right by him and the next thing he did was to look at his money to see if he had got enough to buy some hens. and when he looked he had just enough and so he went strate away and bought some hens to put in the hen house.

and when he had bought the hens he thought of something els and he thought of building a well and so he bought some bricks with his money and started to buld a well with them and it took **him** a **very long** time to buld the well and he got very tired so he had a rest and something to eat and drink and then went out and started to get on with the well and while he was bulding the well he thought about his farther and how he died untill he had nearly finished and then he had his tea and finished the well. then he said he will get some water and fill the well up with it and got a proper well.

Here is something very different going on. So different that it is important to make it clear that this story is very like all the other stories in certain ways, though no two children wrote about the same characters or events, and the features which make this story so different from the diaries are shared to a lesser or greater extent by all the stories.

In the first place it is very long, though it is by no means the longest. All the children's stories are longer than anything else they write.

In the second place, the sense that a story is something long and full makes entirely different demands on their language resources, and brings within reach language forms to fit the needs of an extended narrative; and they know this because they are familiar with stories. This writing is not just written down speech.

Ian's story, for instance, is not about things as they are but as they might be; it is about thoughts and feelings and reasons and speculations. He wrote:

> ... one day he (the farmer's son) heard of some men coming round building things for people and *he said to himself* I'll ask these men to build me a hen house and *be happy. and perhaps there wouldnt be* any need to have anything else on the farm *because* the farm *might be* full of animals, *but if not he might* buy more sheep to put in the cattle shed ... *but if* there is too much on the farm *then he would* sell some and *might be even richer* ...

Here he is dealing with *possibilities*, and possibilities can only exist in the mind. His story is only partially structured by the chronological order of events as they happened. In order to cope *explicitly* with possibilities he has to use 'the complex internal organization that language itself provides for representing relations of sequence and hierarchy and consequence'. This is a long way from the simple narrative pattern in the diaries of things as they happened.

Furthermore, to show that this greater richness and

complexity is a function of story-writing and not an individual difference here is Ian's diary entry for May 5th:

> On Saturday we went to watch my daddy play
> criket ... and while we were watching Me and
> My brother went to watch the bowling and while
> we were watching the bowling a boy came up
> to us and we made friends with him and his name
> was neal and I got my ball and played football
> and my brother was in goal and after one of us
> had got ten goals we played criket with the boys
> bat and ball and then we had diner and then we
> played football for a bit and then it started to rain
> and so we went home.

This differs little from the other diary entries; its pattern of events is chiefly strung together by 'and' and 'then', and it makes no attempt to verbalize his feelings.

In the third place, stories deal with another aspect of possibility at an altogether different level. The characters and events make a *symbolic* representation of how things might be ... 'Once upon a time there was a guinea pig ...'; 'One day there lived a farmers son ...' When they are freed from the constraints of the actual, as they are in story-writing, the children explore all sorts of possible patterns that events might take. Their stories are shaped to their desires and fears, and like dramatic play allow them to verbalize symbolically areas of experience which are impossible for them to express in explicit form. One boy, for instance, wrote two stories and a further whole book about two children (or two animals) who went walking and could not find their way home. As the children's preoccupations change, so the themes of their stories change. Preoccupations are, of course, states of feeling and these determine the events of the story, but in addition the children feel it appropriate and necessary to make explicit reference to how their characters felt. Ian says:

> 'the farmers son *felt very proud*.... but he *was*

not satisfied because he wanted some hens ...
I'll ask thees men to buld me a hen house and
buy some hens and *be happy*.... at this he was *so
happy that he danced all round the farm* ... it
was a *very nice dream.*'

In the fourth place, the stories show the children's
language moving from the expressive towards the poetic.
They are much more shaped than written down speech,
in that they show formal elements. These seven-year-olds
are quite clear that they are writing stories, and that
stories are recognizable and exist 'out there'. Sometimes they head their writing—'My Story'; often they
make a more ambitious superscription such as,

The Car that Talked
Written by Mark Tolley
Pictures by Mark Tolley
Published by Mrs. Thompson.

Their past experience of literature is in the background
all the time; they were familiar with stories before they
could write—I am not, of course, suggesting conscious
imitation, only that they have a notion of what stories
are like from their past experience of listening to stories,
and equally they know that they are now engaged in
writing a story.

They begin in the way they expect stories to begin:
'One day there lived a boy ...'; 'Once upon a time there
lived a little girl ...'; 'Once upon a time it happened
that ...'; 'Once there lived a rabbit ...'; 'Once upon a
time there was a man and he was a carpenter ...' The
formula 'One day there lived ...' may seem a little odd;
probably we should regard it as a broad verbal gesture
indicating that a story is about to begin—the formula
sounds like the beginning of a story and has no exact
meaning.

The other formal element which characterizes the
stories is the repetition of situation. Consider Ian's story
quoted above; first his account of what he wanted, then
his dream in which he got it, then his transformation of

the dream into reality—all dealing with hens and a hen house. David's story shows this patterning element even more clearly:

> One day there lived a boy his name was peter and he liked pets and he had a fish, a dog, a cat, a rabbit and one day he went to bed and in the morning his fish was dead so he went to bed the next morning he found out that his Dog was dead *he was very sad* so he went to bed and the next morning he found that his cat was dead so he went to bed and he found that his rabbit was dead and he had to save his pocket money and he got a cat first and then he got a fish and then got a dog and then got a rabbit last of all and he was not sad he was glad that he had pocket money and he only just had enough pocket money to buy all he wanted.

It looks as if the formal beginnings and the repetitions of events are features that make a story recognizable—'this is how it goes'. Few of them are concerned to end their stories unless 'they all lived happily ever after' fits what they want to say, and a good few of them lose their grasp of their individual 'construct'—the pattern of events that they *wanted* to make—and slip back into the pattern of what happened yesterday. What they write then looks very like an extended diary item. Nicola, for instance, writes a very long story that begins:

> Once upon a time there was a guinea pig and he lived in a shop with lots of other guinea pigs ... and a little girl and her mummy came in ... (they buy the guinea pig and take it home) ... and Jane played with her toys and her Mummy did some washing up and then Janes Mummy made the tea and then Mummy brought the dinner in and when they had finished Mummy washed up the dishes and then she put them away....

This goes on for eight more pages and the guinea pig is

mentioned only once (four pages later) when she goes to feed him before she goes to school. Her language is still tied to the memory of actual experience; she cannot dissociate it enough from *actual* past situations to improvise about *possible* situations as can the other children whose work has been quoted.

In contrast with this, here is Mary's story (one of her diary items is on page 61). She is completely in control of what she wants to say and is able to take a familiar story as her starting point and improvise upon it to produce her own version:

> Once upon a time it happened that a little Foal
> was boran at a farm. It was a black foal the only
> white was a star on his forehead. He was a *very
> happy* Foal at the farm untill his mother died of
> a very bad disease. Everybody *was sad* because
> she was a very good horse. A few years later
> when he was a grown horse he was sold to a girl
> who *thought he was mavles* She teached him how
> to trot canter and Jump and all the things a good
> horse should know then they tried to think of
> a name. At last one of the family said I think
> Black Beauty would be a good name dont you.
> yes said the girl whose name was Alice yes I do
> So his name was Black Beauty.

This story is a long way from speech—'it happened that ...'; 'when he was a grown horse ...'; 'she teached him how to *trot canter and Jump* and all the things a good horse should know ...'; 'At last one of the family said ...' Moreover she is beginning to use punctuation. Her sense that she is making a construct in the written language is more fully realized than many of the others'. Right at the other extreme is what Andrew wrote in his diary entry for May 5th:

> Monday May 5th I am going to play at digers and
> I will have my tip loding car and I am going
> to have my big pece of rok will go have my big
> lorys out and I will dig and I will have my soligs

67

(soldiers) as werk men and I will dig deeper and deeper in the ground and I will triy and make a big hole and the solidigs will then make a hut for then to live in and I will make a tunal in the tunal will be a shelten from a avalanche and ther will be Balke mis for the men to look in the pit and ther will be a big lory will be a garag and the soligs will have to make a big gun will go to the owory and dow all the things that ned blowing up.

This seems to be a written version of the kind of running commentary that young children often speak aloud as they play with their toys; but because it is written, not spoken, and because the boys are not actually there, Andrew writes his story in the future. Most of the children's diaries are concerned with real events. To Andrew this imagined situation is more important and operates more powerfully than the actual events of his life. This is the sole news item for May 5th. His entry for the next day is very similar. Adult criteria of written language are inappropriate in writing such as this. The power and tenacity of imaginative play are something to be remembered in planning activities which foster children's learning.

Mathematics and science: moving towards the referential
The language of mathematical and scientific items in the children's books is not self-initiated; a general pattern has been formulated by the teacher and is clearly intended to provide the basic form which will report each child's specific findings, i.e. to accommodate *individual* discoveries and *common* conclusions. Under the heading 'Mathematics' Timothy wrote:

My pencil measures 7 inches
My book measures 8 inches downways, 13 inches half cross ways
My longest finger measures 3 inches
My shortest finger measures 2 inches
My thumb measures 2 inches
I am 39 inches round my head.

All the children who wrote about measuring had measured whatever they liked, but all had set down their findings in this way.

Again, 10 of the children had chosen to work on a graph (histogram) to show preferences of various kinds. The work of all is headed 'Graph to show favourite ....' (pets, flowers, pop groups, etc.). They have been shown how to set out the graph and record people's preferences, and how to state the results. Here are David's results:

> 14 people like Everton
> 3 people like Liverpool
> 10 people like Wolves
> 4 people like West Brom
> The favourites are Everton
> *They are fantastic*

And Mary wrote:

> From my graph I can tell that there are 13 people who like dogs. ther are 3 people who like cats. ther are 3 people who like rabbits. ther is 1 person who likes guinea pigs, there are 0 people who like hamsters.

> *I think it is a sheme for hamsters Because they are suche nice creahs*

Clearly, in this work the mode of setting out, and the pre-ordained impersonal language for recording their findings, is part of the ideas that the teacher is leading them into. She had provided them (loosely) with the referential language model of the adult world, but these seven-year-olds make their impersonal recordings of the preferences of their class mates and sometimes add comments that are purely expressive. In these transitional writings one has, as it were, caught the language on its way from being very like speech to becoming very like a particular form of adult writing which is almost purely referential. One has also caught a glimpse of the *way* in which information is assimilated; it is immediately brought to the bar of individual evaluation; past experience and present feelings sweep in to help incorporate this chunk of objective information into existing views of how things are:— 'Everton are fantastic'; '... hamsters are such nice creahs'. Later such evaluations will be edited out as irrelevant, but at this stage I suggest they are performing a fundamental role in learning by enabling the young writer to relate his new knowledge to himself.

Impersonal writing

The other set of writings that all the children did were reports of experiments with air. The first one is headed 'All about Air'—a promising title—but the experiments seem to have taken on something of the character of a conjuring performance. Yvonne wrote:

> All about air
> Air is invisible
> Air takes up space
> we put a handkerchief
> in a Jar and it did
> not get wet because
> it had Air in the Jar

She continues:

> Warm air rises
> [diagram]
> we put lit paper in a
> Jar and we put a
> piece of cardboard
> under neath the Jar
> and we put another
> Jar under neath the
> other side and the
> somke rises

All the reports of the experiments are similar to this.

None of them conveys the sense that the children have entered into and understood what they are doing—as their reports of measuring and of making graphs did; none of them contains the expressive elements which indicate that they are making this new learning their own.

Piaget's well-known experiment in which the young children thought that a tall thin jar held more water than a short fat jar even when he poured the liquid straight from one to another is startling evidence that children of this age cannot grasp this kind of reasoning. The very idea of a scientific experiment involves setting up the situation in such a way that only one explanation is possible; i.e. to rule out all alternative possibilities. It is precisely this mode of thinking that Piaget believes to be beyond the powers of young children. It seems likely that these meaningless reports reflect the mumbo-jumbo appearance of the experiments to the children. Children do learn what the world is like from observation—smoke rises from chimneys, bonfires, cigarettes and forbidden matches; they feel draughts and rushing wind and fly kites, but they neither require nor can cope with the kind of verification that controlled experiment is aimed at.

Furthermore, this particular work in science, concerned as it is with generalization (air takes up space; warm air rises) raises some very sharp issues that go beyond the Junior School. There are many important notions which we could never arrive at from our own experiences. These notions are presented to us by other people (teachers and books). Vygotsky calls these scientific or non-spontaneous concepts, and in order to make them our own—to grasp them—we have to make them grow downwards into our personal experiences which they can then unify and generalize; we turn the unfamiliar into the familiar by referring it to our representation of the world *as we have experienced* it. It would seem, therefore, that when a teacher is presenting children with generalizations, such as those quoted above, it is crucial to include interpretation in terms of their own familair experiences as part of what is being learned. If children are encouraged to report their early scientific work in the impersonal and generalized mode adopted by adults and by convention widely used throughout the secondary school, they are being prevented from using the most effective means by which these difficult and important areas of knowledge can be learnt. We shall see later how the ten-year-olds cope with science, but when experimental work is appropriate it should surely follow the lines of the Nuffield Junior scientific work which encourages the children to be explicit in all sorts of ways about their responses to observation, experiment and prediction. The more abstract and generalized the notions, the more important become the interpretations from personal experience: the children need the opportunity to refer their new learning to 'their representations of the world as they have experienced it'.

Other items

I now want to consider the things the children wrote which were in no way directed. Ian and Jill each had 23 different items in their books; others had 21, 19, 17 and so on down to 9. These covered expressive letters to Mrs. Thompson, observations of animals, birds or treasured objects, what they called 'newspaper articles' but were in fact stories starting from something in a newspaper; there was an account of the Romans in Britain, and a report of how milk bottles are crated. There were some poems and occasionally there were brief items copied from newspapers. Clearly any first hand or secondary experience that interested them might be matter for writing. Such freedom of choice results in different kinds of writing beginning to appear. Where specific topics are set, as is the general pattern in secondary schools, such choices are not available and there may be a consequent loss of flexibility of language and even loss of the capacity to write in tentative or exploratory ways.

Language learning is a matter of improvising upon 'models' and gradually becoming aware that you are doing so. Speech takes its differing forms from actual situations; thus talk to strangers is different from talk with familiars, and talk with a friend of the same age is different from talk with a friendly adult; talk with a parent is different from talk with your Headmistress, even when it is Mrs. Thompson. When speech begins to be written down, it very early reflects the differences of situations, and the different language models that surround the children begin to affect how they write, just as speech situations affect their talk. I have referred to the children's clear sense that a story (or a poem) is something 'out there', a construct that you make with words, and that this sense can only come from their familiarity with literature.

It is not so easy to trace other models but one can say that the children have a sense of available forms. One knows that the impersonal mode is rarely a part of their language experience at this age, yet it does occur in their writing. Two boys wrote identical pieces about crating milk—it followed some arithmetic about pints and quarts of milk. Nicholas and Mark wrote:

When the milk *is taken* to the dairy on milk lorrys
it is got out of the crates by a big graber and
then *it is taken* to a big machinin that washes it
and then they dry it and *it is time to fill* the
bottles again and then *they have there tops on*
then the graber puts them back in the crates.

This is the only instance of the passive voice in all the writing and it is perhaps significant to see how confusing it is to the writers. The use of 'it' and the passive make them lose their sense of the grammatical subject. At first 'it' refers to the milk but it rapidly becomes the bottles and when they write 'it is time to fill the bottles again' this new 'it' disrupts the structure and with some relief they revert to the active voice—'then the graber puts them back in the crate'. This is not a kind of language they are familiar with yet. I suspect that this is untransmuted secondary experience; had it been firsthand experience I think it would have been described as they saw it and the language would have been much more sure.

When Ian writes about the Romans, even though he is dealing with secondary experience, he makes it entirely his own. He writes:

> Many years ago when the roamans lived they bult
> long strate roads and very good buildings because
> they were civilised people and very clever and
> strong and one day when the roamans knew a
> very lot about England they said to thereselfs we
> will go to that countery and so they made
> very strong boats and sailed across the sea but they
> had to have many fights before they came to
> England and when they came to England some
> people who were already there wernt very strong
> so some ran away to Wales and some ran away
> to Scotland but some stayed and joyend on to
> the romans army and the romans invayded
> ingland for two thousand years ....'

It is interesting to compare this self-chosen account with pieces in other classes set by the teacher as a test. The orientation is different, Ian assumes that what interests him will interest his reader, so in writing about these past events he has shaped the facts to his own order and view of the world with a different purpose from that of the test situation.

In addition to the varying kinds of language that children encounter in the course of their lives at home and at school, there are the specific models that people teach them. I have quoted instances of these earlier in this article in commenting on the children's writing in mathematics and science; some of the poems written would also come in this category of taught models, since a generalized notion of a poem as something that rhymes at all cost is very widespread.

As one looks at the writings based on taught models one is struck by their relative lack of success compared with what the children learn for themselves by encountering all sorts of language experience and using what they feel to be appropriate as they go about their daily occupations.

B. The eleven-year-olds: a week's work

The school

The work of this class came from 34 children, 16 boys and 18 girls, mostly aged eleven (or nearly eleven) in a County Primary School in a recently developed area of Staffordshire. This school, like the last one, has an informal way of operating; children and teachers talk to each other informally a great deal; the Headmaster, when he can, sits down to talk to the children as he goes round the school; there are new books set about the place, tanks of fish, exhibitions of poems, stories, pictures and things made.

In looking at the work of eleven-year-olds in this school we were asking the same question as before: 'What are the children using their language for?' but we chose a school that was very much like the Infants school in its policy, i.e. informal talk, books—including a lot of literature—and a large measure of self-directed work were dominant features. In neither school were the classes streamed.

The writings

The teacher's notes for this class of 34 children show that the starting point for all the writings was a common one, i.e. none of the work was self-initiated, but given a common starting point the children took off in all sorts of varied directions. The starting points in this week's work were:

(i) Something felt, seen or heard during the holiday (May 1st);

(ii) The history of May Day celebrations;

(iii) Mathematics: children were asked to record measurements without using rulers, etc.: history of thumbs, cubits and yards: the need for standard measurements—decimal system;

(iv) Radio-vision (wireless commentary and film strip of the Great Barrier Reef) accounts written; work on a communal frieze;

(v) Reports of what they had read this week;

(vi) Friday answers to general knowledge questions given on Monday;

(vii) Pond Dipping or Pond Discovery;

(viii) First chapter read of *Stories of King Arthur and his Knights*: children wrote dialogue or stories; scrap paper used for play-writing—it gave more expressiveness and informality;

(ix) Discussion on hunting: film on stag hunting talked about: extracts read from *Tarka the Otter*: fox hunting and beagling discussed (beagling from first hand experience): *To see the rabbit* by Alan Brownjohn was read; the children then wrote in any way they liked.

In addition, the children chose any piece they liked from their English book and copied it; (their own writing—some chose to copy poems they had written).

As one would expect with children in their last year in the Primary school, there is a great increase in the amount of secondary experience, but although there is a common starting point in topic, information, film, literature, etc., there is no expectation that there will be a common finishing point, that all will need to have learnt exactly the same things. In fact the reverse is true; the children clearly expect that they will proceed in their own directions in their own ways. There is no attempt to impose any particular form on how they write or display their work except that they mount it on white sheets of paper so there is a sense that it should look good and have drawings and pictures as well as writing —hence their teacher's remark about doing their plays on scrap paper when she wants the focus on getting the language down without attention to presentation. The teacher helps them as much as they want while they are writing but no corrections at all are made on the actual work.

The results of this freedom to write and explore as they wish are twofold: first they do not edit out the expressive features of their writing when dealing with the referential—pond life for instance, or the Great Barrier

Reef—in an attempt to attain objectivity. Their writing includes their subjective response to their exploration of the world around. Articulating their response is a step towards self-awareness. Cassirer says, 'If I put out the light of my own personal experience, I cannot see and I cannot judge the experience of others' (*Essay on Man*). This remains true of all new experience (or learning) at whatever age it is encountered.

Second, and this is really a consequence of the first, the children write in all sorts of ways. They are sensitive to the language that they meet in books and from their teachers and one can see the influence of the 'models' they are meeting reflected in their work. Had they all been taught a particular way to write their science (or geography?—Great Barrier Reef) this exploration of different modes would not have happened. Both expressive elements and variety of modes are illustrated below.

Moving towards the referential: participant language
Mathematics. Neil's measurements are recorded as follows:

> Length of desk=14 half thums
> Width of desk=16 half thums
> 21 Neil thums=1 Neil cubit
> 2 Neil cubits=2′ 8″
> 33″=a nose to tip of finger yard
> 1 Neil foot=9″

And Anita wrote:

> The width of my desk is=16 thumbs
> The length of my desk is=16½ thumbs
> *I used my thumb*
> 28 Anita thumbs=a Anita cubit
> 2 Anita cubits=26¾ inches ...

—and from here to the need for standard measurements and the decimal system. 'I used my thumb,' Anita records, and it is plain to see that an Anita cubit takes more

Anita thumbs than does a Neil cubit, Neil thumbs. Individual measurements and expressive elements in the records bring the notion of a standard measure into their personal experience.

The importance of primary experience as the basis of learning is an axiom in this school and the children's own formulations of things they have done, seen and felt is regarded as an aspect of primary experience. I want now to look at three other pieces of work that the children did in this sample week which were all concerned with new information derived from secondary experience; I want to look at the way it was related to their first-hand experience and then to look at the various ways they dealt with it.

First, then, the way it was presented to the children:

1. Junior science (variously headed—Pond Dipping; Pond Discovery, etc.) (See item vii above.) This work was based on a pond-dipping expedition; the children were told how to approach a pond, how to net the creatures, how they caught and ate their prey, how a fish breathes, etc. This provided a rich body of information rooted in first hand experience; no one was in any doubt, for instance, about what a water scorpion looked like (observation) or how it ate its prey (information).

2. The Great Barrier Reef of Australia. Work on this was based on a film with commentary, together with discussion and re-showings of parts of the film to reinforce questions and discussion. The children wrote about it and made a frieze. Thus, though not first hand experience, they saw what corals looked like and observed in the film the fish and other creatures that inhabited the reef. Many of them reported that they 'made corals' to go on the communal frieze. This work again gave a rich body of new information which the visuals brought very near to first hand experience.

3. The history of May Day celebrations. This was dependent on the teachers' words; it was history and remote from their own experience so it had to be recreated in each child's mind by the interpretation he was able to

put on the teacher's words. They were then invited to write either a report or to write about May Day as if they had been present at the celebrations in some particular place. Where they chose to write as if they had been present ('My name is Arthur. I am going to tell you about May Day ...') they made it clear that they had understood this was a holiday in some sense like the special days they know themselves—Easter Monday for instance; where they wrote about it as history it tended to be a random collection of facts ('On the first day of May there was always rejoicings in the villages from as far back as the twelfth century. There were rejoicings on May Day in the Bible. The villagers lived in cold huts all the winter,' etc.).

Those who wrote about May Day as if they had been present at the events they had been told about were able to give their account the coherence of a story and they were able to interpret the facts in terms of people's behaviour which was, of course, what the teacher was chiefly hoping for. But there is another point at issue. Not all kinds of information lend themselves to this treatment, and this raises sharply the problems of dealing with informational matter in writing. Here is this body of new information together with those parts of one's experience which relate to it. How does one set about engaging with it? Theoretically one can take any bit of it and start there —and this is what these children do; but once started, where does one go? Adults solve this problem in general, in terms of purpose and audience (as I am attempting to do in this article), and in particular by means of generalizations which provide the 'skeleton' of the writing.

The situation, however, is different for children. They do not usually see themselves as explaining things to adults; they do not argue much in writing; they do not usually ask questions and try to answer them in writing, and they don't give instructions in writing. Their role is usually to receive instructions. So how are they to set about structuring informational material that they are asked to write about? Where do they begin, and where are they to go?

In the secondary school one of the commonest purposes of writing is 'to show that they know what the lesson was about'—a test situation in fact, with the teacher as the audience. Within this general direction the teacher usually structures what they are to write by giving a title or a question to be answered: 'Industry and Farming in the South West of England' or 'Becket's quarrel with Henry II'. This, of course, is also often the procedure in Primary schools, but not always. In this class the children make their own titles to indicate what they are going to write about and they are free to describe and comment on whatever they like; any selection of facts and comments and any order that they may choose to impose are equally welcome—i.e. importance is placed upon the choice they make. This is not therefore a test situation; it is a situation of mutual trust and respect. But the children's freedom to move about as they wish within the subject matter does mean that their selection of items is eclectic, depending on what has caught their interest, and until they can begin to use generalizations, what they write inevitably has this random character. The writings of these eleven-year-olds where it is explicitly concerned with the world around them is very like the writing of the seven-year-olds in this respect, but one can begin to see the growing ability to use generalization and abstraction as a means of organization: 'A pond can be very interesting, most people do not know what is among all the mud at the bottom' or 'Limestone is coral's skeleton and its house'. This is the development of conceptual thinking at work, and it is by this kind of thinking that they will learn to select and order referential material, but it is a late development, and we have plenty of evidence that generalizations imposed by the teacher are often meaningless to the children.

Let us now see how these children attempted to solve this problem of structuring their referential writing. Since this was an unstreamed class, there are big differences in the amounts and the quality of what was written.

The first thing one observes about the writing of this class is that it is all more or less expressive; there is no sense that any of the writing (except perhaps the

Mathematics) should be written in any given way, yet one can observe all sorts of background models influencing what they write. Only their accounts of their holidays are relatively uninfluenced by adult forms of writing; they are like speech or informal letters, and they differ from the personal writings of the seven-year-olds only in the enormous extension in the areas of experience that they verbalize. They are no longer little bald pieces but detailed representations of major and minor events in their lives. For example, Lyn wrote a piece that she called 'A Few Days in the Garden'; here is part of it:

> ... 'Let's get the chairs out and play at houses'
> said Joycelin. We made two little houses. Soon
> it was dinner time. After dinner we went to a
> bunglo with Joycelins daddy. He mowed the lawns
> while we made daisy chains. We made a daisy
> chain that was as long as the bedroom and half
> as long again. Then we went to the bathroom.
> We both sat in the bath. Joycelin crept out and
> told me to go to sleep. She put the tap on and
> wet my clothes. Her daddy came in so we hid
> in the cupboard....

In the other pieces (items ii to ix above) nearly all of them are trying out all sorts of other 'voices' which they feel are appropriate according to the 'stance' they have taken up in their inner dialogue. This is particularly clear in the writings that are moving towards the referential— 'Pond Dipping', or the 'Barrier Reef' or 'May Day'.

Here is what Lyn wrote; she bounces up like a puppy dog and says:

> Do you know what this is? A pond is the answer
> (coloured picture). Fish (coloured drawing). Water
> Spider (coloured drawing). These are just two
> of the things that live in the pond. Of course there
> are more things. A fish breathes through its mouth
> and can only live in water. So if you get a fish out
> of water it will of course die. Like we would die
> if we were put in water for a long while and could

not come out. A water spider lives in a bubble
of air underneath the water (picture). A spider
can also run across the water without getting its
feet wet. (Coloured drawing) This has a caddis fly
inside.

This is very much as she would speak, and she tells
only the items that interest her.

Sheila writes:

> It is all very interesting getting ready to go Pond
> Dipping with tins, jars and nets. When you get to
> the pond children shout, talk and frighten the
> fish away before they even start dipping. Afterwards
> when the talking has stopped, cast your nets in the
> water. About two minutes later lift your net out.
> Empty your catch in a tray, a white one *is best*.
> If you have a Pond Book with you, *it is a good idea*
> to look up some of your catch....

This is a very different 'voice' from Lyn's; is it perhaps
the teacher's tones that she has caught ('... a white one
is best....' and '... it is a good idea....')?

Here is another voice, Robert Farmer. This one begins
with a rather surprising generalization, but he fails to
use it to provide a framework for his piece—which has
a consciously bookish and humorous tone:

> A pond can be anywhere, behind trees by the
> railway almost anywhere you think of there is
> likely to be a pond. When you have found a pond
> unknown to you and I the thousands of little
> creatures go into exile, they hide under stones
> under weeds and in the mud. One of the most
> interesting creatures in the pond is the water spider
> which spins a web under water and then gradully
> it takes down air and stores it in the new home
> it has built.
>   Another interesting creature is the Caddis fly
> larvae this is am interesting creature because it is
> a tasty meal for any animal who feels a little peckish.

But nature gave this creature sense to build a house of anything it can find wood, little stones, dead leaves, this provides protection against its enemys.

Then there is Martin's piece; he too feels it appropriate to begin with a generalization: 'A pond is a small lake filled by vegertion.' (I think 'vegertion' means plants *and* animals to him). 'Tadpoles, Sticklebacks and minowes are some of the most common ones.'

Unlike most of the children he does not choose the most *interesting* creatures to describe but follows up his second generalization about the most *common* ones. He continues with a third generalization which he develops:

Dragon flys are the enemy of most insects in the pond: when they are young they proul around like cats to catch insects.

He then goes on to describe the family life of sticklebacks. We can see in this account the beginning of the adult pattern of weaving in and out of the general and the particular. But this is no imposed pattern: 'Dragon flys are the enemies of most insects in the pond. When they are young they proul around like cats ...' Here is his own experience, his own language rooting his generalization in the particular.

Now let us look at what Neil Hackett writes; he heads his piece 'Science'. This I think is a pointer to how he thinks about it—yet another model, and a familiar one this time:

In the pond there are many different kinds of creatures. Fish are a certain shape so that they can get through the water fast. They *are said* to be streamlined. *It is best when pond dipping* to put plant eating insects in one tank and meat eating insects in another. Caddis flies make their houses with anything they can get their feelers on....

Although he has the scientific 'voice' with its detached

tone and impersonal phrases, his piece lacks any structuring in relation to the general statements that he begins by using, and his last item is pure speech. Up to that point he is imitating a model without *using* it.

And here is a very adult 'voice'; Robert Lim writes:

> *A pond is full of life. A whole city in miniature may exist in a pond. The animals in the pond are either carniverous or vegetarian.* The carnivors are meat eaters and the vegetarians eat plants. *Of all the things* which live in the ponds the caddis fly larvae *is the one with the best camaflage.* It makes *a kind of shed out of the substance around it.* (drawing: caddis fly)
> The water spider has *an ingenious method* of breathing under water. He makes his den and then he brings down air bubbles in his hind legs! (drawing: water spider)
> The fish breath by breathing in water and then *extracting its properties of oxygen by means of a type of grid.* (drawing)

His first paragraph shows generalizations being *used to structure* all the items in the paragraph. I think by 'city in miniature' he is getting at the idea of an underwater community with its carnivors and vegetarians, and with carnivors around some of the creatures will need camouflage. Then he goes on to describe *methods* of breathing. His items are not random; to be concerned with *methods* of breathing under water implies a hierarchy of related ideas which is altogether different from Lyn's egocentrically interested report that water spiders can run across the water without getting their feet wet. Robert is deliberately and skilfully using a particular form of the written language, but he is not afraid to make his own improvisations when he needs to—'a kind of shed ...' and '... and brings down air bubbles in his hind legs!' These improvisations reveal the crucial process of relating new phenomena to his existing knowledge.

Finally, somewhere between Lyn's and Robert's is Neal Jackson who wrote:

What kind of world is a fish world? Imagine living in water all the time. There are many kinds of insects which crawl about the weeds and mud. Many are *unearthly like creatures*. Illustrated opposite is a caddis larvae made up of *bits and bobs* such as sticks and stones. Also there is the water scorpion which kills its enemys. First it kills them and then sucks out all the juices. Fish are streamlined for swimming. They breathe by swallowing water and extracting the oxygen from the water and pushing it out through his gills.

Neil hovers uncertainly between the personal and the impersonal; he cannot yet manage Robert's level but he is on the way to it and he improvises with similar felicity. His piece is essentially coherent because he structures it throughout towards his starting question—'What kind of world is a fish world?' and towards his answer to that question—'Many are unearthly like creatures.'

In this loosely graded selection of writing one can see individual assimilation and shaping in the choice of items and the choice of 'voice' to write in; but one can also see the beginnings of attempts to find a means of structuring—a general idea which will make sense of the scatter of particulars that follow. This groping for unifying concepts is a marked feature of the children's referential writing in this class.

I think two points arise from this set of writing. First, when children are free to select and order as they wish, they are also free to draw consciously—as Robert does —or unconsciously, on the language resources that are in their inner ears from their reading, from television viewing and from their teachers, and it is worth noting that in this set of work there were 34 different 'voices'. If they are taught a particular way of writing and are asked to recapitulate what they have been taught in a lesson, they cannot draw freely on these resources; neither can they attempt to shape what they write, and shaping in referential writing is *thinking* itself. In these 34 free pieces we can see all sorts of 'models' being tried out. In other words, this same freedom allows them to use language creatively as a tool of understanding. At the points where they attempt to relate the new to their existing knowledge they improvise in terms of their own experience, and this is the only sure foundation for learning. ('Unearthly like creatures'; 'a kind of shed'; 'bits and bobs such as sticks and stones'; 'limestone is coral's skeleton and its house'.)

Second, and rather a different kind of point, because they are allowed to use language as an adult is free to do—without injunction—we are able to see the process of selecting and ordering at work.

The stories and poems: spectator language: moving towards the poetic

Both the stories and the poems are very different from those of the seven-year-olds. The obvious formal elements in both have disappeared. No one begins 'Once upon a time', or 'Once there lived ...'; none of the stories has the repetitive patterning of events that is familiar in fairy tales and legends: but their basic purpose seems to be the same—the exploration of the possibilities of human behaviour, possibilities that are shaped by the children's notions of how they would like things to be, or more rarely, how they fear things might be. The stories *seem* more realistic, less like fables or fairy tales, but although the peripheral details and settings and conversations may be realistic, the central pattern of events reveals that the children are still more concerned with how they feel about things than with how things are. Every child except one, for instance, makes his hunted creature either escape or die a quick death. (Item ix in the list of work done in the sample week.) They are not concerned with the realities of the *events* of the hunt but with the different realities of the emotions of the hunter, or of the hunted or of their own preoccupations in disguise. So, instead of the obvious formal elements these stories are shaped by an interior coherence which arises from the stance that the writers adopt. Lyn writes:

Hello my name is Tinker I am a little puppy

86

dog.... I'm not really a huntsdog but I sneak out and join in....

From then on her story is determined by what she sees and how she feels as a puppy dog sneaking out to join in the hunt. The seven-year-olds were not capable of this kind of interior coherence arising from the possibility of being someone else for a time.

Let us look for a moment at the complex tissue of possibilities that any narrative presents to a writer and try to see to what extent these children can take account of these. A writer is a spectator of imagined events and in spinning the web of his story he draws on his own experience and his experience of literature. First there is the pattern of events in all their fullness. Neal begins:

The dogs split as they came through woods followed by about a dozen horsemen. They stumbled over a hillock squealing and barking. The dogs, mostly terriers and hounds jumped over a rickerty old stone wall except for the smaller dogs who tried to find a detour.

Here he is the narrator observing the scene from outside, as it were. A mature writer does not give equal weight and value to every item that he describes. He turns a kind of spotlight on some and represents them fully in words, as Neal has done in his opening. Other events are reported by a brief statement; Neil writes, 'Everybody saw their quarry, a fox'. Here the spotlight has been turned off but the thread of the narrative has been maintained and we are ready for the next bit of highlighting. In addition to the writer's bird's eye view of what is happening, he often interrupts his narrative to explain why something happened or why someone behaved as he did. Neal says, 'The fox was taking a chance in trying to beat the dogs to the causeway'; and Robert says about his chief hound, '... getting overconfident he went over the stream'. This is still the voice of the narrator but he has moved his focus from description of events to comment and explanation. But these areas are only part of all that is happening—which is the potential province of the writer. He may want to concern himself with how the hunters felt and their view of what was happening, or how the hunted creature felt. A mature writer may take any or all of these elements into his purview; what most of the children do is to take up a single clearly defined stance and structure what they write from this viewpoint—'My name is Snish,' writes Martin, 'I'm a dog. I'm a Scotty dog. Whenever the hunt comes I join in ...', while Susan begins, 'It was a warm day and I was happily looking after my cubs ...' Most of the children write in the first person; some of them use only monologue—a story consisting entirely of speech-like utterances, like Martin's above. This is limiting, since it does not allow the writer to comment or shift his focus as a narrator. He is really a character in a play without the play. Others, like Susan, write a narrative in the first person—the story of a vixen and her cubs and the hunt; there is no conversation, only the events and the thoughts of a confused and frightened creature. There is little sense of writing for anyone but herself. As in dramatic play, she *is* the mother fox. Hilary, on the other hand, declares herself aware that she is writing a story in every sentence. She knows the conventions of stories, and the conventions of writing them, i.e. of punctuation and paragraphing, and she seems to enjoy it immensely. She wrote:

The keeper opened the door of the kennels on that chilly morning. I sniffed in expectation. 'Not today chum' was all he said. I tried to make my inside do a nice deep rumble. 'No' he said, kindly but firmly—'it's the hunt! You'll enjoy that, eh boy?' I wagged my tail. 'My inside say somfin's happenin today Mum,' I said. 'You cannot,' was the prim replie 'depend on an inside, especially one like yours.' I slunk into a corner, tail between legs remembering the grass for the ponies I had chewed, 'but', she continued, 'as it happens it is THE hunt today and you're to attend.'
    'Grrrrr! Gruff! Rufar! Grrr! Silly old horses

Grrrrr.' 'Will you stop gowling!' barked an old
hound, 'they help us!' I slunk away. The horn
sounded and I thundered along with the others.
Suddenly Canlly our champion hound picked up
the scent. The horn sounded again. 'To horse!
To horse!' We stampeded after fox. 'Hullo you're
new' said a friendly hound. 'First hunt' I replied
proudly. 'It's great fun isn't it' he said. 'Lovely'
I said 'jus' like I've always dreamed.' We streamed
downhill, the wind in our faces, silky ears flapping,
noses twitching but Canlly way ahead. We came
to a river and stopped. Canlly sniffed uncertainly.
I ventured toward him—but this was easy the
scent was clear as day I bounded along after it.
'Gosh look at that pup go' said the head hunter,
'we've found another Canlly—Great!'

  I was petted praised etc. After it all I said
triumphantly 'well Mum even with an inside like
mine you can tell a "somfin' funny day"!'

The keeper very rapidly changes his sex and turns
into her mother, but the young hound triumphs and wins
the argument as well. I think this story, like most of
them, and like all the stories of the seven-year-olds is
really about the writer. The events—in this case a hunt—
and the characters—provide the symbolic framework
within which the writer makes a coherent image of a
bit of life as she would like it to be.

It is interesting to see how Robert (cf. p. 84) feels
about these matters, who was so markedly superior in
his referential writing. His sympathies are all with the
hounds—and these were no ordinary dogs. They were
specially reared alsatians with red eyes, and the best is
called Scarlet Streak. He uses the third person and writes:

The dogs barked and snarled. Then, Woddle,
who was an old hand at the game, barked, jumped
up high and charged forward. They had 'found'
the scent. These were no ordinary dogs. They
were specially reared alsatians. They all plumeted
forward, knowing that the scent was that of a fox.

The next five minutes were the fox's last. Knowing that he could not outrun the mighty alsatians, he crossed a stream and then crossed back to the side from which he had come. Because Woddle had first found the scent the others decided that he was shrewd and that they would follow him. Woddle, getting overconfident went over the stream. The others followed. All except Scarlet Streak. He did not see Woddle and Co. but went over another stream after the fox. After some time (1 minute) Woddle and Co followed. In one minute the fox fell, a bite through the brain.

This story is accompanied by drawings of splendid alsatians with red eyes and tongues. It is pretty much of a fairy story in spite of the sophistication of his language. Like Hilary he is aware throughout that it is the written language and a story. Every sentence declares him a reader and a confident improviser in language. What is it really about? I think it is about alsatians and the way he feels about them. I think that all the children, no less than the seven-year-olds, turn the framework of events to their own ends. Here is what Neil Hackett wrote, the only story with a sad ending; perhaps it was a story he had read. Nevertheless this is what he chose to write about. It is a different kind of hunt from all the others:

Kotic was a seal. He had a big scar on his back. When he was two years old he was driven to the fur farm inland. One man said fire and in a few moments Kotic could not recognize any of his friends. They had all been skinned. Kotic just ran as fast as he could back to the beach but he could not. Desperately he ran round trying to get out, then a man walked up to him. Seeing the scar on Kotic's back the man flung him carelessly out of the enclosure. At that moment Kotic fainted.

When he came to his senses Kotic was in great pain. He had broken his flipper. Very soon as he lay on the beach dieng he thought that men could have taken his skin anyway because they will probably take it when I am dead.

In writing about the slaughter of the seals he has distanced it somewhat. Thus it would seem that in writing their stories the children are not only exploring the possibilities of other people's and other creatures' lives, but also giving shape to aspects of their own lives, particularly their feelings.

It will be remembered that the language of the seven-year-olds' stories was very much more complex than that of their referential writing and I suggested that this was because dealing with possibilities inherent in fiction makes greater demands than dealing with simple actualities. When we come to look at this aspect of the writing of the eleven-year-olds we find a more complicated situation. First, in story writing, the children do not always choose a model which allows them to make use of the language resources that they have. The monologue is an example of this. In these cases the writers' referential pieces show more advanced forms. Second, generalization and conceptual thinking are beginning to appear in the children's referential writing and this means that they are developing forms of language that are *potentially* as powerful and complex—though different—as the language of imagination. Most children, however, do not realize this potential, and their referential writing remains a scatter of dissociated items, whereas their stories are structured by narrative form, by their feelings and by their own experience. So for most children stories (and poems) are the means by which they use language most effectively and comprehensively.

For comparison here is Neal Jackson's story together with his account of the Great Barrier Reef. It is worth noting the words he uses in each, the types of sentences demanded by the relatively simple itemized account of the Reef and the complexity of the various viewpoints he covers in his story.

The Great Barrier Reef

The 'Barrier Reef' is really little sea creatures. They are called pollyp. The Reef is on the North East coast of Australia. Often the coral forms coral islands.

These islands soon have a huge growth brought in by wood and birds.

There are many kinds and colours of coral. There is 'Stag horn', 'Dancing Lady'.

Often people go hunting on the coral and it is advised to wear pumps to safeguard against the many creatures who live in the coral.

Going back to the coral islands many creatures live there. Such as turtles who often lay a 100 to 200 eggs. When they hatch there is a mad scurry to the sea and usually only five get to the sea because of marauding birds.

The Fox Hunter

The dogs split as they came through the woods followed by about a dozen horsemen. They stumbled over a hillock squealing and barking. The dogs mostly terriers and hounds jumped over a rickerty old stone wall except for the smaller dogs who tried to find a detour.

Then everybody saw their quarry a fox. A few blows on a horn from the head hunter and the dogs split into groups. One group heading to cut the fox off by a causeway over a shallow stream. The other pack encircling the field on the fox's other side, the horsemen would cover another side and the only route opened was up a drive leading to a farm. The fox was taking a chance by trying to beat the dogs to the causeway. Somehow the fox reached the causeway and ambled over. He must have escaped.

Suddenly there was a shot which brought dog man and horse to a stop. In front of them lay the fox breathing his last breath. To the hunters right a scruffy looking farmer held a double barreled shot gun which was smoking in his arm.

'Had to get the little old critter before he got
to old Bess and her little chicks.'
He turned and walked off.
The hunter blew his horn. They turned their
horses and headed back the way they had come.
Dogs stumbling after them.

Though in this week's work only a few poems appear,
it is clear that the children read and write a good deal
of poetry. The stereotyped notion of a poem as something that rhymes at all cost does not appear and the
expressive language that is found in all that they write
has probably the greatest scope in the poems, but there
are not enough of them in the sample to make more
detailed comment.

Peter wrote:

Lobo

Lobo the wolf slinking along
Lobo's feet soft and padded
But at the tip are claws of death
Which can kill a deer with one swipe
And its jaws full of gleaming teeth
Which can break a man's backbone
You might think he's nice, out of action
But if you harm his mate watch out
because the white snarling lump of danger
will descend for the kill
You wont have time to shoot
you just try and fight with your bare hands.

It should perhaps be noted that there was in this
week's work no self-initiated writing as there was in the
work from the seven-year-olds. With the eleven-year-olds
all that they wrote arose from a common experience,
from which they pursued their own directions. We do not
therefore know whether the common starting point in
the literature read that week *provided scope* for the
children's preoccupations which they would not otherwise have found, or whether the theme of the hunt

prevented some of them from writing about preferred areas of experience. What is clear is that Alan Brownjohn's poem 'To see the Rabbit' produced several imitations so close to the original that they seemed to have little relation to the children's own experience. This raises the question of whether referential and spectator writing might not have different starting points. The referential must at some point work towards that which is held in common. This would seem never to be the need in spectator writing which realizes the individual's satisfaction as a 'maker'. Literature is clearly of crucial importance, but perhaps it should not be too near to the children's writing in time, or too directly linked by the teacher to what they are about to write.

C. The nine-year-olds: a week's work

The school

The work of this class came from 26 children, 11 boys and 15 girls aged nine to ten in a primary school in an industrial town of 50,000 inhabitants. The town expanded from a village in the 1920s, so that much of the housing is modern (post-1920), but few of the children's parents have any roots in the place; they have come, over the years, from Scotland and the North of England to work in the new industries. The school itself is the old village school, a pre-World War I building situated near the industrial zone. It is old-fashioned in that it has a fixed time-table for lessons, much formal instruction, a good deal of copying of material and set exercises, and there is in this class no extended work based on first-hand experience, and little opportunity for self chosen writing or other work. The teacher of this class was probably the most informal in the school. Each year group of the school is streamed into three classes, of which this is one of the two lower ones.

The writings

Each child in this class had done 25 to 30 items and a good many crayon pictures, but their books were very much school exercise books, with a fair sprinkling of red ink corrections. There was no sense, as there was with the eleven-year-olds, of something made, and mounted and illustrated. The books contained a great deal of scrappy, non-continuous writing such as word lists, spelling lists, answers to questions given orally, items set out in numbered sentences (e.g. How Jesus turned the water into wine), and half a page of arithmetic—just figures, meaningless as they appear in the books. At any point between these items poems appeared, copied or made up, between 6 and 10 of these in most books. Between 10 and 12 of the items were concerned with the work the children were doing that week on telling the time. This included making a clock face with movable hands, answering questions every day about time, one piece of continuous informational writing about ways of telling time in the past, and poems about clocks.

In addition to this work on 'time' and all the other miscellaneous exercises, there were 5 pieces of continuous writing which all the children did; all these were directly related to work done in lessons. They were:

(i) How you got in touch with someone by telephone;
(ii) A report of a radio lesson on how we hear sounds together with drawings of the structure of the ear;
(iii) An imagined account of travel in Tudor times;
(iv) How Jesus calmed the waves;
(v) The reproduction of a fable about the sun and the wind.

Over and above all the directed work (some 670 items for the class as a whole), there were 8 pieces of self chosen writing—4 brief accounts of personal experiences and 4 stories—and in addition, 8 children copied out items of information which interested them.

It needs to be noted that there was almost no self chosen work in the class discussed in Section B (eleven-year-olds), in that almost everything they wrote arose from some common starting point: i.e. their writing was also related to work done in lessons. But, given a common starting point they then diverged in 34 different directions even when the starting point was an informational one.

I have suggested that these divergences arose from the teacher's expectation that they would pursue their own individual lines of enquiry and that with this in mind they were provided with a rich and varied matrix of common experience to start from. In the class now under discussion, among the items (i) to (v) listed above, only items (i) and (iii) allowed the children to take individual directions within narrow limits; the other three demanded a set pattern of events—sheer reproduction in fact.

If we ask the same question that we asked before—what are these children doing in their writing?—we have to reply that in most of their work they are reproducing things that they have learned in their lessons, showing their teacher that they have learned them. Richard summarizes it for us:

> when we where having lessons this morning we lernt about time and we lernd about a.m. and p.m. and that am is in the morning and pm menes in the after-noon. and we have lernt time-table time and that clock wise mens the same way as the clock gows and anti clockwise mines the opposite way to the clock.

Since most of the writing of this class is very near to speech, perhaps the most useful way of looking at it will therefore be to try to trace the points at which it moves away towards other models.

The seven-year-olds and the eleven-year-olds were given opportunity and encouragement in verbalizing their individual experiences—their day to day living, their fantasy and their new experiences arising from work at school. Out of all the writing done by these nine-year-olds (Class C) there were only *four* pieces concerned with personal experience. Two were about visits to the circus; here is one of them. Senga wrote:

> One day daddy came home with four tickets for the circus. daddy are we going to the circus I said yes we all are said daddy we are going to night. Oh goody goody I said. we all better get ready

now my mummy said So off we went. At the circus
people where coming in and sitting down, then a
lady said the trapeze boys It was good fun looking
at them next it was red nose the clown with his
pet monkey He was very funny the circus was good
I said and my mummy said it was good too.

This is very like the way she would speak and is very
little shaped by a sense of the occasion: there is more
focus on the events leading up to the circus than on the
circus itself. It is expressive and carries a sense of her
feelings about the whole situation.

Here is another of the four pieces, written by Linda
Cummings:

Play Time

I went to see if my friend was coming out to play
with me and so I went to see If she was coming
out She was coming out so we had a game of
hide and seek together and then my mummy said
come in and get your tea and then I had to go to
the shop for my mum and she gave me sixpence
to spend and then I came home and I went out
to play again I played shopping with my friend
and I had to go in because my Mum said and then
I had to watch television for an hour and then I
had to go to bed.

This, like the previous one, is structured only by the
sequence of events as they happened. It is much nearer
the writing of the seven-year-olds in general than it is to
that of the eleven-year-olds in general. This is written
down speech with the elements connected by 'and' and
'then'. If this piece of Linda's is put alongside the story
by Nicola, aged seven, on p. 66 and also alongside the
piece by Lyn, aged eleven, *A Few Days in the Garden*
on p. 81, we can now see at all three age levels the most
elementary form of the written language being used; if
there were no other work to look at it would be difficult
to guess the ages of these three children. But both the

older children *can* use other modes, though Lyn from Class B, with a rich school experience and much feed-in from literature does not go beyond speech models as yet (her piece about Pond Life is quoted on pp. 81/2). Linda at nine (from Class C) and with much more limited opportunities for varied writing can move into another mode, though it looks as if her work in general is well beneath her capabilities because of the restricted nature of the curriculum. Here is what she wrote about travel in Tudor times:

> In the Tudor days more of the people *travelled about towns* on horseback and the roads were very bumpy and very bad. The farmers took big heavy stones out of the roads and there was big holes as well ... The king and the queen *spent much of their time* going round the country. *When it was known* the king and queen were visiting towns folk they hurried very very very quickly to mend there roads and queen Elizabeth had more waggons than anyone. She had for hundred waggons all together when she went on her journeys.

Here is a mixture of her own speech model beginning to be modified by the teacher's language and possibly by books. Her writing here has moved towards the referential.

The rest of the writings in Linda's book are either exercises or reproductions so she had no other chances to try her hand at real writing, no opportunity to use her own language to help her learning.

If we now look at the four stories we find that three of them are about mysterious or alarming night occurrences. They are brief and have moved only marginally towards the poetic—they begin and end as stories might be expected to do. For example Timothy wrote:

A Scare

One night on a Friday at 12 o'clock I was very thirsty so I got up for a drink of water and heard

a scream so I went to my bedroom window and
I saw a big man with a beg on his back it was a
burgaw. So I called 999 for the police ....

There follows another paragraph of the same length in
which the police catch the burglar. But Linda Harman
wrote a different kind of story which is reproduced in
full for several reasons. It is not written down speech.
Linda has a sense that she is writing a story and it is the
only clear instance of this in the whole class. She knows
some of the conventions of the written language—full
stops and capital letters, for instance, and the way she
uses dialogue shows some influence from children's
stories of the Enid Blyton type.

The Things that Jane and Sally saw

When Jane and Sally woke up the curtains where
drawn back and the sun was shining in the bedroom.
'O' look at the sun it is as bright as as every
said Jane and Sally. Just then there mummy came
in. Mummy mummy look at the sun it is ever so
shiney. Yes I no said mummy. What have you
got in your hands said Jane. "O'" yes I have
been up the shops when you where sleeping and
bort you a new dress each. Can we wear them
today said Sally. Yes said mummy that's how I
have brought them up. When there Mummy showd
them the dress that she had bought them they
said 'O' they are very nice said Jane and Sally
and they put them on. Are you ready said there
mother. Yes gust coming said Jane and Sally. 'O'
you look pretty said there mother. Where going
for a walk before we go to school. What do you
want to go for a walk for. Our teacher told us to
try and get some flowers for the classroom. Well
you havn't got time to go to the woods so you can
go round the farm to see if you can find some
flowers there. So Jane and Sally went out to look
for some flowers in there farm. When they got
out of the house, all they could see was long green
grass and lose of pretty flowers. 'O' aren't they

lovely said Jane. 'O' yes they are the most lovelyes flowers I have ever seen said Sally. There was roses and daisies daffodils and lilys and tulips and panseys. Jane and Sally took 5 of each of the flowers. Then there mother came out it is time for school so off they went. When the teacher saw them she said thank you and put them in water.

This is, I think, a fantasy in spite of its seeming to be concerned with realistic things such as new dresses and flowers for the teacher. I suggest it is an arrangement of imagined events as Linda would like them to be—a shadowy friend who can scarcely be distinguished from the writer, a new dress, praise (how pretty you look), being allowed to pick the best flowers from the garden, the teacher's gratitude. So, in this respect, Linda is doing in her story what all the other writers were doing, making a satisfactory pattern from imagined events, re-arranging life as it might be, and this, of course, is what professional story writers do too. Judging by the rest of the work in the children's books—though it is easy to misjudge in having only the books to look at—she has not been encouraged to express her own responses to things, so she has fallen back on this particular literary model with its stereotyped and unexpressive dialogue—another case of starved capabilities. Compare this with seven-year-old Mary's account of the incident with Mrs. Bowaller on p. 61. It is significant that this story of Linda Harman's is the longest piece written by any of the Class C children, with one exception which I shall come to later. Children need enough opportunities to write stories— and need enough stories to read—for them to develop the sense (which the seven-year-olds so clearly had) that a story is something 'out there', something made. In this class, this story—dull though it seems—is the only one which exhibits this sense, but there were only four written. In order to compare the work of this class with that of the other two classes I have had to focus on the four pieces of any length and quality. A survey of the whole range of work is more conclusively revealing than the individual examples I have quoted.

Although there is little evidence of prose literature in the children's writing there are many poems scattered about in their books. Some of these are copied and some are made up but it is clear that although they like the poems that they copy—many have illustrated them for instance—the poems that they write are no more than word games in which the need to find rhymes drives out sense. For instance, Steven writes:

I went to bed
And saw a man
He had a pram
And he had a red thing on his head.

I went under my cover
Because I thought he was a goast
And I told my brother
And he had some toast.

And John wrote:

I go to school every day
And I want to play
And it was the middle of may
And that was the end of the day.

All of them are like this, so the poems that they write are not expressions of felt experience. One could contrast with these the poem *Lobo* on p. 93.

There remains for comment only the copied pieces. Most of these are about what one might expect—types of aeroplane, inspection pits in a garage, a bus conductor's ticket machine, Roman bridges, Christopher Columbus ... items that may reflect the children's interests or merely some available material to copy; they are all brief except one, and this one stands out by its length and by the fact that the boy kept it up during three days, writing it before and after the interruptions that his set work clearly constitute. The handwriting is beautiful and it occupies five full pages, much the greatest amount that anyone wrote. It is the only language of quality and imagination (including the poems) that can be found in all the books. Here is part of it:

Wasps

The Buzzing can be heard in gardens and fields in
summer time and autumn. The wasps are looking
for nectar in the flowers. They settle on fruit
in the orchards and suck the sweet juice. Bees
may be flying there too. The wasps are a brighter
yellow and smoother than the bees.... The wasp
has two very large eyes. On her head also are
two long black feelers. With these she can smell
and feel her way about ... Only the queen lives
through the cold winter. She sleeps or hibernates
in a sheltered place. It may be the bark of a tree
or under some dry leaves. On a warm day in spring
the queen wasp wakes. She crawls out into the
sunshine and spreads her wings. She feeds on
nectar from the flowers. Then she looks round
for somewhere to build a new nest. The queen
wasp may find a hole left by a field mouse or a
mole ....

and so on to the end of the cycle of life of the wasp. Judging only on what is in the children's books, starvation of imagination is hardly too strong a term to use: beside such a diet this piece is a rich feast. One other boy also copied part of this passage.

To summarize the chief differences between the writings of this class and those of the other two classes: most of the writing is discontinuous—lists, sentences, etc.; there is a lack of first-hand experience, and no attempt to get the children to use their own language to explore new experience; there is little impact from literature and an absence of imaginative writing of any sort; they have very little opportunity of choice since so much of their writing is closely tied to recapitulating information from lessons. It is quite likely that the social environment is less favourable than that of the other two classes, but we know from evidence from other schools where the children come from homes with limited backgrounds that exploration of the physical environment at first hand can result in writing of a quality and quantity which does not begin to be reached by these children. Expressive work hardly appears in these books; there is much incoherent and non-continuous referential writing, and there is little movement towards the poetic.

But there is a postscript.

A set of large paintings came in as part of the week's work. These arose from class discussion about the relative costs and advantages of different kinds of transport, and each child had written a few lines about his picture on a square of lined paper and stuck it on one corner. While this rather spoilt the paintings it also allowed them to have an effect on the writing, and because the pictures were much more directly related to first hand experience than was the class discussion a little crop of expressive and imaginative writings appeared on the stuck-on slips; for example:

> I am the Driver of a big plane ... it is very hard when we go up through a cloud and it is very hard work when we land as well....

> I am a fruit lady and I go around the doors selling my fruit

> One day my daddy gave me a ride in a car transporter ....

> My dad works in Golden Wonder. He drives a lorry load of crisps .... But my dad gets a good wage. He likes the job.

> I'm moving today Hurray Hurray
> The time has come today
> I'm moving today Hurray Hurray
> I'm moving to Scotland today today.

I have tried in this study to draw out, from a detailed

examination of all the written work done in one particular week, some very general points about children's language; but the writings that form the sample can only give a partial picture and the study is not intended as a critical comparison of teaching methods in the three classes, though any such study implies consideration of the teaching in the background.

The question, 'What are children up to in their writing?' implies, of course, that children do not write just to practise writing. At one level they are simply co-operating with their teachers—doing what they are asked to do, but over and above this, they seem to be engaged on the one hand in handling *information*, reporting things about the world around, sometimes in their own terms and sometimes in language taken over from their teachers or from books; on the other hand they seem to be using their writing to improvise upon experience for the fun of doing so, to explore the possibilities of experience, to enjoy—that is to say—experience they have not had. These two directions in their writing correspond to the distinction that James Britton makes between language in the role of spectator, which he defines as one of the characteristics of literature, and language in the role of participant which is language used for some practical end. Clearly one kind often shades into the other, especially in the writing of younger children, but the striking difference between their stories and all their other writing suggests a difference in function arising from a different relationship between the writer and his situation. The children's accounts of preferences for pets or football teams, of how we hear sounds or of how Jesus calmed the waves were for the purpose of reporting and recording and explaining, whereas their stories were symbolic representation of their inner preoccupations and interests. The distinction is important because it enables us to see how literature and personal and imaginative writing on the one hand, and writing that is concerned with knowledge in its generally accepted sense on the other are complementary, and that both need to be fostered. The importance of participant writing is self-evident; children cannot advance in school education without it. The importance of language in the role of spectator is not so obvious because it is not directly related to practical ends. Yet in terms of its function in children's development it can be seen to be of the utmost importance.

Within the writing in the spectator mode we find both autobiographical and fictional (or fantasy) stories. The first are important because they establish the validity of children's own experience now, for themselves and in the eyes of their teachers; this is the creative milieu. The second—the area of fantasy—is the only mode by which children can give utterance to areas of experience which are most powerful but which they cannot be explicit about—their fears, anxieties, griefs, hopes, excitements and pre-occupations. These can only be represented symbolically and this is what the stories are really about. Sometimes the characters are mothers and fathers and boys and girls, sometimes animals, sometimes farmers or shopkeepers or taximen, sometimes old men or witches or giants—the disguise is significant—and the 'persons' and events play out the concerns of the writers. Fantasy, whether expressed in dramatic play or in stories or pictures is the only mode open to young children to interpret their most powerful experiences. Blake says,

> The child's toys and the old man's reasons
> Are the fruit of the two seasons.

Yet the power of fantasy never ceases to surprise. Vygotsky's comment that the motives for writing are often far from children is, I think, true for writing in the role of participant. Writing to report or argue or explain often looms as a task, but fantasy has its roots in emotion and dream and is powerful enough to overcome the physical labour of writing and the distractions of angry adults calling for attention and action. Furthermore, the scope of stories makes possible all sorts of extension of language, and the writing of children with experience of literature reflects these extensions.

It seems appropriate to end with a story which embodies most of the theoretical ideas expressed in this article. Stephen Tolley wrote a letter to a visiting teacher to explain why his work was late. He is eleven and in his first term in his secondary school. He wrote:

Dear Mrs. Smith
My monster is late because I did not finish it in English and I only had a cuple of lines to do and I finished it off in geography so my house tutor mister mordred taw it up and I had to take it home and do it. I hope you like it from Stephen Tolley yours faithily.

With the letter came his 'monster'—the second one, which he had done at home. The middle of the page was a picture of a visionary monster with flames shooting from his scaly purple head and a 'long strong' orange tail. Above and below the picture was his story. The picture was not an illustration; the picture and the story round it was a construct of imagination; the words said:

Fier Cali

He has rough hard scales like a crocodiles on his head, a body like a great lizard and legs like a dragon and a long strong tail. He has butiful coulers and he breafees out flames. I once went into a cave with a river running through. I did not know about the monster I just walked in. I saw a flame round a bend and I was practically paralised. When I saw the monster I turned and ran as fast as possible. I was speechless but I went back again.

by
Stephen T.

His regular English teacher said about the incident:

Anyway Stephen cried and wouldn't really be consoled by 5.30 p.m. when I saw him. However I gave him a stamped addressed envelope so that he can do it again if he wants to.

Stephen's letter is a piece of writing with a practical aim. Its function is to explain why his work was not done. It is also, I think, to maintain his relationship with the new teacher. It is participant writing because he wants it to affect the course of events.

His 'monster' as he calls it—his construct of imagination—has no such practical purpose. He had accepted the teacher's request to write about a monster and had made the task his own. From then on, its purpose lay in the satisfaction of making it, and in his assumption that the teacher would share his satisfaction—this is language in the role of spectator.

Language, the Learner and the School, (Penguin), by Douglas Barnes, James Britton and Harold Rosen, is an important book about classroom interaction whose concerns complement and overlap with Miss Martin's—as the following quotations show (see also pages 204/5 below):

> In the 1967 lessons [a sample of five across the curriculum] there was not one example of an 'open question not calling for reasoning'. This would match teachers' impressions that those children who come up from primary schools ready to explore personal experience aloud and to offer anecdotal contributions to discussion cease to do so within a few weeks of arrival. Clearly they learn in certain lessons that anecdotes are held by the teacher to be irrelevant. (page 25)

> If the lessons of the sample are typical in this respect, teachers might well question their own attitudes and behaviour in the classroom. Are they teaching their younger pupils that to learn is to accept factual material passively and reproduce it for matching against the teacher's model, to be judged right or wrong? ... (page 27)

> ... It might be surmised that these pupils are not only learning about Palestine but also about the kinds of reciprocal behaviour appropriate to a teacher-pupil relationship, that is, learning when not to think. (It should be remembered that they are in their sixth week in a new school.) (pages 33/4)

In his essay, 'Poetry and the Inward Life', in *Presenting Poetry* (edited by Thomas Blackburn) (Methuen), David Holbrook writes:

108

Verse form in poetry, choruses, repeated phrases, rhyme, like musical restatement, inversion and such repeat patterns as in rondo form, enact the constructive gain over the chaos of experience by reassuring us of continuity ... Rhymes, rhythmic patterns and stanza-form fortify the deeply satisfying sense of 'this comes round again and I recognise it: I feel continuity: I shall survive' ... This reaction explains the great happiness children feel for repeated rhymes they know, and their conservatism, in clinging to known poems and rhymes ... (page 72)

The next article complements, rather than disputes, such a view. It concentrates on one wing—the 'Poetic'—of Professor Britton's model, and can be seen as a sort of appendix to Miss Martin's article.

‖‖‖

WRITING POETRY IN THE CLASSROOM

Jeremy Mulford

'Poetic form' may simply mean 'the rules' (for instance, a particular rhyme-scheme) or it may have a much less limited meaning, such as James Britton gives it when he refers to '... the *formal* characteristics of the utterance, and in particular its coherence, unity, wholeness'. It is my contention that, properly viewed, the first is but an element of the second. Form as defined by Professor Britton is of a piece with meaning: he is not concerned with 'shape' or 'coherence' or 'wholeness' except as having to do with meaning; and the form, in the limited sense, of a poem may contribute both to its local meanings and to its wholeness.

A concern with formal rules *for their own sake* will always be trivial. The rules that Alexander Pope followed in writing his heroic couplets, or the even more rigorous rules to which Racine submitted when writing his Alexandrines, have no significance except in so far as adherence to them contributed to—or limited—the scope and meaning of the poetry. For example, rhyme may intensify or, indeed, create a significant relationship between two words; or, in a more general way, it may embody an attitude of the poet towards his subject—thus, Pope's use of rhyme in relation to rhythm helps to establish the authority, the confidence, that is characteristic of much of his verse. To take a different sort of example: because Racine's rules are so restrictive, the merest variation within the uniformity that they impose takes on a significance which, otherwise, would not exist, or at least would not be noticed. (Similarly, because of the convention of preternaturally slow movement in Japanese Noh plays, the slightest quickening of pace has meaning; and the very occasional sudden violence of movement is all the more shocking.) These are but a few instances of adherence to formal rules working for meaning.

One of the problems for the teacher, concerned with children reading and especially writing poetry, is how to prevent them reaching the notion that poetry largely amounts to the rules. Here, Professor Britton's addition to Sapir's two categories acts as both a salutary reminder and a guide. In his concluding quotation, obviously it is an inner unifying impulse that is determining the pattern, not any prescribed, formal rule. If Professor Britton is right—I am sure he is—that this is not a freak example, but representative of a tendency common among children, then here is a phenomenon to which all teachers should be alive. And if, when children write their own poetry, they have an undue concern with what they take to be the rules, this will preclude the possibility of shape and pattern having meaning. It is depressing to be told by a class of ten-year-olds that a poem by Arthur Waley is not poetry because it does not rhyme. It is even more depressing to find that the staple of a class's poetry writing is such as Nancy Martin quotes on page 101. This is to imply not that any harm is *necessarily* done if children play with rhythms and rhymes for their own sake; but that care should be taken that they do not come to an early notion of poetry that is arbitrarily and debilitatingly exclusive.

The ten-year-old boy who wrote a poem beginning

> The sun drops o'er the dusky moor,
>   In purple, blue and gold,
> Many a time the earth hath seen
>   This sight, for she is old.

had an unusual sensitivity to words—that is clear. However, although one cannot be sure how much he was involved in writing the poem, it seems likely that he would have been more so if he had had different models and a different notion of 'the rules' in mind. The nine-year-old girl who wrote

> Where the green grass
> Shivers in the cold cold wind,
> A man and a boy with no money to spare,
> They leave the city at day and seek for shelter at
>   night.

The quiet quiet countryside makes them feel afraid.
At night an owl will hoot loudly and the trees
make deadly shadows.
A rabbit will scuttle away as there foot-steps sound.

had *her* models too (in particular, 'The Little Cart',
translated by Arthur Waley from the Chinese) and *her*
notion of the rules (poetry need not—and on this occasion
must not*—rhyme); but this is an example of how an
inner impulse towards order has fused with an external
rule to produce a poem which, though derivative, is
personal. The way the writer conveys throughout the
poem the ambivalence of her attitude to the natural world
makes it seem certain that she was fully involved.

In both pieces, we may see how the diction and movement of the model or models stand similarly to the
rules in relation to the inner impulse. In the first, not only
rhyme and regularity of rhythm but also archaicism
have tended to usurp personal apprehension; whereas in
the second, both the rule of no rhyme and Waley's spare
gentle rhetoric have been assimilated. The main conclusion to be drawn from this is certainly not that
unrhyming poetry only, and preferably Arthur Waley's,
should be put before children.† Rather, it is that they
should be given only good poetry—that is, meaningful
poetry—as varied as possible. (It is difficult not to believe
that the boy had read or heard much bad verse, and of
a limited kind. At the same time, there can be no doubt
that if the girl had continued to write influenced only by
Arthur Waley, her poetry would soon have become
mannered and empty.)

Generally speaking, the fewer and less restrictive the
rules are that a child feels it necessary or desirable to

---

* I had suggested that she might try writing a poem containing no
rhymes at all.

† A friend has suggested that anybody who happened to read
my essay in Denys Thompson's *Directions in the Teaching of English*
(C.U.P.), where I also make particular reference to Arthur Waley,
might get an impression contrary to this. Perhaps I had better
emphasise, then, that I refer to him often only because he is peculiarly
useful as an example, since it is usually quite clear when a child is
being influenced by him.

112

follow, the more likely it is that what he writes will be meaningful. On the other hand, a desire to submit, in some measure, to an external form can often foster the tendency that Professor Britton describes. Here is an acrostic by a ten-year-old boy:

*F*rogs hopping about on lilly leaves on a small pond.
*R*uling the small pond as if they were kings and
                      queens and high people.
*O*r playing mums and dads, well thats whats
                they looked as if they were playing.
*G*oing crocke, crocke very softly and there large
                  eyes hardly winked.
*S*lowly they one by one dived under the water
             so I went home and told my mum.

This, I think, is a good example of *collaboration* with a particular form. The 'inner impulse' is noticeable both in the modulation from 'hopping' and 'Ruling' to 'very softly', 'hardly winked' and 'Slowly' (the word has a rightness about it, even though it is perhaps not fully accurate), and in the gradual shift towards a self-orientation ('as if they were ...'—'well thats whats they looked as if ...'—'so I went home and told my mum').

It is probable that the ten-year-old boy who wrote the next poem was hardly conscious of there being a problem of where to break a line and begin another (I had not mentioned the matter). Nevertheless, one can feel an incipient sense of technique at work, under the impulse to say something personally important.

My Dream

I glide through the air
Like a dove, I go through
A cloud, I choke, it gets in my throat.

I feel a cold chill as I
Go over a mountain I see a little
Bee that sits on my back.

113

I start to get tired so
I go to an oak tree and
I sit in it while I get my breath back.

I start to go home, I feel a
Chill—that mountain again.
I say goodbye to Bee and go home.

I wake up next morning. I say
To my mother 'I had a dream that I flew!'
'Don't be daft boy and get washed.'

The poem has a memorable unity. But it seems likely that the unifying impulse was vulnerable—that, had the boy felt obliged to write in rhyme because that was the rule, the sureness of movement towards the abrupt anti-climax, which gives the poem its unity, would have been absent.

There may be a case for a teacher banning rhyme on one or two occasions, and there is a strong case for *suggesting* that children might try writing poetry without it, especially when they have very limited preconceptions about what constitutes poetry. But a ban might well itself amount to an unwarranted imposition. Provided that a child has experienced a wide variety of poetry, both with and without rhyme, it is better to leave him to *decide* in what form he wants to write; for only when he does not feel that he has to work to a prescription will his inner impulse be free to organise what he writes. My last example is by a boy who (unlike the last three children quoted) passed the eleven-plus, but whose writing was usually dull. He wrote the poem, quite unsolicited, several weeks after I had read the class some poems by Arthur Waley, and we had discussed them a little.

A War

The beggars walk along the dusty road,
When a man calls them to him to help him load.
The man says, 'Why aren't you going away?'
'Because we want to stay.'

'But there is a war on in this world.'
'But we were not told.'

I don't know why he wrote this poem (we had not been discussing war), but clearly he needed to; and the influence of Waley's poetry, its characteristic spareness of statement, enabled him to control what he wanted to 'represent'—the wholeness, on this occasion, being a function of the selectivity, of what was left out. But, it seems, *he also needed the rhymes.* At the same time, since he was not writing to any prescription, he did not feel obliged to end with a perfect rhyme; and this contributes, in a small way, to the poem's prevailing quality. The poem may not be memorable *as a poem*, except in being a child's performance; but, to my mind, the boy was writing *as a poet.*

Note: for further comment on teachers' influence on children's attitudes to poetry, with particular reference to teacher training, see pages 213/9 below.

In his essay, 'Poetry and the Inward Life', referred to on page 108, Mr. Holbrook has much to say of importance about poetry, even for the reader who finds his more specifically Kleinian language unhelpful. Such a reader may find Nancy Martin's piece a little later in the same volume, entitled 'Children Writing Poetry', more to his taste: it has general preoccupations that are similar or related to Mr. Holbrook's.

Although Emmeline Garnett's note on anthologies, also in the same volume, is about books for the secondary school, its concerns are very relevant to the primary school teacher. Miss Garnett hesitates between two positions:

> Unfortunately, from even a cursory glance at the publishers' lists it is clear that most of what they offer is pre-digested, and with very little variety about it.

and

> One must not be too unkind. There are many good anthologies ...

But her main drift is towards a salutary indictment of the anthology industry:

> I would ... suggest that what we have are anthologists fed and reared on school anthologies and making their selection almost entirely from other anthologies. And so the vicious circle goes on getting tighter. And how the publishers succeed in printing four hundred anthologies, and presumably selling them, is a real mystery ...
> The over-riding impression is that with a few noble and notable exceptions, the anthologists do

not really read and enjoy poetry themselves, except from other anthologies.

———

When teachers talk or write about their teaching for the benefit of other teachers, it is right that they should usually select out the best, the most successful parts, in a proselytising spirit: 'This *can* happen: this *did* happen.' But the effect of this will always be, to some extent, to hemeticise the experience and the achievement. A teacher could well come from a reading of, say, Sybil Marshall's *An Experiment in Education*, (C.U.P.), marvelling at what she did with her children but also wondering in a more mundane sense, as to how she managed to do it: 'My children aren't like that' (a statement at once true and untrue).

The problem is especially acute with informal drama. In this case, fear on the part of teachers—fear of chaos—is likely to be at its strongest. To attempt informal drama with children enthusiastically requires, among other things, a firm faith that chaos will not—or, at least, will not *necessarily*—result. Many teachers will not reach this faith until they have actually witnessed it working successfully. Because of this, it is likely that even such classic works as Peter Slade's *Child Drama*, (Univ. London), or books containing much to assist the teacher such as Enid Barr's *From Story into Drama*, (Heinemann), or indeed the article about drama in this book, will influence and help only those teachers who are already well disposed towards their cause. At the same time, to the inexperienced eye, success—especially if it is only partial —is not always self-evident. Thus, in the next article, Ian Burton describes work involving College of Education students and two lecturers (himself and Anthony Jones): to a large extent it was only after the students had returned to college at the end of a session, and were discussing with the lecturers what had happened, that they came to recognize what of positive value had been going on amidst the intermittent disorder (a disorder that was inevitable given the fact that the children were unused to the freedom of informal drama, and that the students could work with them on only one afternoon a week).

We need many more descriptive and analytical accounts of informal drama in action than exist at present. But we need more than that. Since it is not generally possible for teachers who have not had any experience of successful children's drama to work with others who have—in the way that the more fortunate among college students can—there need to be available more drama sessions on film or video-tape: not the sort favoured by the B.B.C. or ITV in which the relationship between teacher and class is so highly developed that all the children seem to be, and perhaps are, absorbed all the time; but ones in which, to begin with, the teacher's successes are very partial and obscured. Such a film, to be really valuable, would have to be long, and it would require at least two (preferably hidden) cameras: one, with a wide-angle lens, to take in the whole class, and another for close-up work. Given such a record to refer to, the teacher's or anybody else's detailed but selective* account of what was happening, written afterwards—his analysis as 'spectator'—would be much more valuable than that account on its own.

———

An environment that is rich in people, talk, stories, books, pictures, our own created work, objects and materials to handle and shape, an environment that provides ample opportunity for adventurous play, is vital in stimulating responses and language in children. Beyond the environment provided by the teacher, the child knows a world of his own—an undifferentiated, apparently haphazard, flux of experience. How does the teacher relate himself, and the environment he provides and creates with the children, to this wider experience? Ian

* Of course, any film must be selective, too; but not in the same way, or to the same extent.

Burton's article looks tentatively at the borderland between the spontaneous play of the child's private world and the more organized experience of classroom drama.

||||||||||||||||||||||||||||||||||||||||||||||||||||||||||||||||||||||||||||||||||||||||||||||||||||||

A DRAGON CAN BE A GIFT

Ian Burton

Very young children's dramatic play in the Wendy House, or in boats, cars and palaces made up of boxes or building units, is self-absorbed; it runs by itself, it is completely unselfconscious, and only occasionally does it need an audience. When it takes on external structures, these tend to be in the form, very close to the nursery rhyme, of singing games such as 'Fair Rosa' and 'The Farmer's in his Den'. These games have strong rhythms in speech and song, strong characters and plot (sometimes hinting at greater complexities), with most of the children participating as chorus and, in the Greek manner, the dramatis personae limited to two or three characters. Movement and grouping will be formal—as, for example, when the chorus circles around 'poor Mary' who 'is a'weeping' in the centre. And through some process of selection or chance individuals in the game change their roles from time to time.

In many Infant schools this natural tendency to dramatic play is encouraged and enriched in the classroom by the provision of time, space, and stimulating materials, and the creation of an atmosphere of trust. But from the 'top infants' onwards this kind of play-drama seems to die out as a classroom activity. Is this because the need and the capacity for it diminish, or because teachers feel less able to provide time, space and facilities? Or is it because children increasingly wish to keep their play away from the physical presence of adults? There is certainly no shortage of valuable and satisfying drama that can be done with *older* Junior children—those of ten and eleven years of age: group play making, for example, based on direct observation of the world around, or dramatic extension of poem and story. Such work seems often to require some kind of audience—or at least the prospect of one—whether it is an audience from the class itself, or other classes from the school, or a larger audience of friends, parents and teachers. But we are less sure of the kind of dramatic activity that is most suitable and valuable to younger children between six and nine years of age. We wondered whether there is a significant relationship between the classroom drama and the spontaneous play and pre-occupations of children of this age, whether there are any clues to be found in their play that might influence the drama that we, as teachers, might do with children.

There is little doubt that dramatic play continues to be central to the lives of most boys and girls throughout the junior and middle school years. It is the constant process of role playing and myth making that is apparent among children in the playground, in the streets, in gardens and parks, on waste ground after the Saturday morning pictures, and at home. The forms and images of this kind of free-wheeling play are often drawn from film and television, from comics and books; the energy and emotions are the children's own, and behind the obvious imitation there is often more going on of their own invention than is apparent to the casual observer. The participants are the only audience.

Does the teacher, armed with her Opie-land guides, have the *right* to encroach on this private territory? What do children of this age need from drama which they do not already supply for themselves? Or, if we accept that classroom drama *is* a valuable activity, what do children invest in it of their private world? On one occasion a class of seven/eight year olds had been doing (among other things) a project on the Bedouin Arab for three or four weeks, and the teacher had asked them, in their groups, to pretend that they were an Arab family and to make up a play about it. When the time came to present these plays and the desks had been pushed back, the first group took the floor and went on interminably with a largely inaudible play in which they seemed totally absorbed. The audience was obviously excluded from their consciousness, but it was possible to discern that they had a tent and a camel by an oasis. They had names like Mustapha and Ali and for part of the time they were engaged in tasks like grinding and winnowing maize. But there was an awful lot of smacking and scolding. Mustapha and Ali were put to bed in disgrace, and Mum and Dad sank down outside the tent, exhausted. The children made it known that they were hungry and thirsty, and, receiving short shrift from their parents, they planned and executed a raid on the biscuit tin in the pantry at the other end of the tent. They were rumbled and beaten yet again, and then the play began to peter out. The children, obviously, were playing out their preoccupation with the conflicts of bed-time which are a feature of the lives of children of this age—especially in high summer.

It was in an attempt to discover how far the play and the classroom drama could be, should be, or inevitably were, interrelated, that a small group of students and tutors from a college of education visited a class of seven/eight year old children for one afternoon a week throughout an Autumn term. We had no intention of going to the children with prepared drama lessons, and in the early stages we did not mention the words 'play', 'acting', 'games', 'drama' at all. The class teacher divided the children into friendship groups of five or six, and each student took a group aside to talk with them. The purpose of the talk was to give the children an opportunity to talk about themselves, their interests, what they liked doing when they were free to choose. Each student introduced himself/herself to her group and the children introduced themselves, and thereafter the talk ranged over a variety of subjects, but a great deal of it was concerned with things seen on television and incidents from books. One might speculate as to why the conversation tended to take this turn, but we shall not digress here to do so— we can only say that our ways into the conversations were as tentative as could be.

In my group (which was in the cloakroom) one girl suddenly announced that, with two or three of her friends, she had made a *play* about Janet and John which they had performed for the class. When she outlined the plot, it was surprising and delightful to discover that from this unpromising material a play had been created involving such unexplained and mysterious events as a dragon hiding in an egg! From this the talk moved on to food and eating, to Jonah and the whale, to Pinocchio in his boat being swallowed by a whale—eating seemed important. The children talked about 'hide-and-seek' and blindfold games—so we decided to play some. In the first game we played, one child sat blindfold with a bunch of keys in front of her. The others had to attempt to steal them. She scanned the group with a pointing finger, and the atmosphere was electric; when the finger stopped, the one it was pointed at was 'out'.

After we had played a few similar games, the group, almost as one, decided to act something they had been watching on television—the making of bread—which had fascinated them the day before. First of all they 'acted' themselves sitting in the classroom, one of them being the teacher telling them to 'sit up and shut up'. The 'teacher' then went over to the imaginary television set and switched it on. At this point the group got up and moved to a different part of the acting area and sat and watched the 'television', while two remained behind representing the television actors talking about, and making, bread. The whole exercise was quite a complex piece of illusion/reality play, involving a mass medium of communication and revolving around the fundamental process of baking the daily bread. They were playing televisions, and this, seemingly, was as important as playing bread making.

During the same afternoon, this group dramatized the story of Chicken-licken, their reading book at that time. This had a circular pattern—more conventional, perhaps, than the television play. It was fundamentally simpler, reminiscent of chain tag. They were all linked together, until they were finally eaten by Fox-lox and the cubs. Being devoured was obviously crucial, and it went on for quite a long time in complete silence.

At the end of the afternoon all the groups came together and we read Kipling's *The Crab who Played with the Sea* to the children—it seemed very appropriate to us with the Eldest Magician allocating to each of the animals his life/play role, but there was never any evidence that the children made explicit connections.

What emerged from this session was that children *do* seem to make mythic patterns out of their own experience—breast-feeding fears as Holbrook might call them, are not too distant from them, and *eating* and its ritualization is important in their plays. They also fall most easily into dramatizing things which have remained with them, or made some striking impression on them, at home or school. They tended to take experiences from the previous day as their source material: we soon discovered that they did not easily remember things from one week to the next.

On our second visit, we tried to follow up some of the things which had emerged, but the children could not remember even who was in which group. Fortunately, the situation was saved by one of the more forceful boys, Harold, shouting out 'Let's do Tarzan!'. Whereupon he divided the rest into chimps, lions and jewel crooks, and we were launched on a whole-class dramatization. He had the chairs put on the tables for trees, transformed the class into a jungle, gave the Tarzan cry, leapt from the table, was set upon by the animals, and a fight ensued which lasted a few minutes longer than was good for our peace of mind. It was not a particularly noisy or disturbing fight—but it was a tangle of bodies much like the tangle game they played in the playground. It was later that the children introduced us to the tangle game: players form a line linking hands, the end player weaves in and out among the bodies drawing the rest of the line after him, until they have formed themselves into a tight and intricate knot, which is then, sometimes, slowly and carefully unravelled without breaking the chain of linked hands. Fighting is not always chaotic in children's play, although there were one or two in this class who always wanted to push it over the edge. On one occasion, for example, when we played circuses, boys did clowning acts in pairs in which they punished one another mercilessly in mime that was highly formalized and controlled —and, we thought, ingenious in its invention.

For plays to turn into brawls is natural and, sometimes, dramatically proper, but some of the students felt that there was a danger of this becoming the fixed pattern, and rather a limiting one at that. So after break we worked some more on the Tarzan story, trying to get plot and some kind of narrative development. A group of girls became tribal villagers, but when we looked more closely at what they were doing in the village, in the corner behind the bookstand, we found they were arranging vases on imaginary sideboards and tweaking at their hair in the mirror, rather than feeding chickens or weaving cloth. The crooks now had a treasure to find, and so the story went on—but somehow without the original élan and excitement.

When we had finished the Tarzan story one of the boys suggested we return to the Chicken-licken story— he had had an idea. He read while the others mimed the circular progress of the chicken and her friends. This was a truly imaginative extension of what we had done before, and it 'worked' extremely well.

In our discussions, during break and at the end of the first afternoon, some of the students expressed alarm at the uncertainty and unpredictability that lay in our experiments at trying to build on what was happening among the children: they wanted to see something 'work', they were looking for *performance*. Certainly we were putting ourselves, and some of the more timid children, at the mercy of the more forceful personalities in the class. So at the end of this second session one of the students told the children a shortened version of the Pinocchio story and suggested that they act it out the following week. We thought that during the coming weeks we would give a variety of different kinds of loose frameworks (like the Tarzan story) within which the children could improvise.

Pinocchio provided quite a lot of material. Inevitably, the story appealed, and when we arrived to work with the children they had already drawn, painted and written things which were related to it. Following one student's suggestion the children acted being puppets in pairs—one pulling the strings and the other being the puppet, one Gepetto, the other Pinocchio. Then one was the Fox and the other the Cat—and so on. Later, there was an attempt to put the various pieces of the narrative together, and it was then that some interesting mythic patterns started floating to the surface. When the Fox

125

and the Cat hung Pinocchio on the tree they quite clearly made gestures suggesting the knocking of nails into the puppet's hands—a 'displaced' crucifixion, in fact. A long newspaper nose on the lying Pinocchio was riotously torn to pieces by the birds.

On another occasion, the story of Noah and his Ark provided not so much a narrative structure as a basic idea on which the children could improvise singly, in small groups, in large groups, as they felt inclined. The children were reminded of the outline of the story and asked how they thought it could be acted out. They pushed the tables into one corner to make a rough platform. On top of this they made the superstructure of the Ark with chairs, and on top of this and under the tables were the animal cages. Harold, who was Noah, bossed his wife about, and his sons and their wives, in language that sounded as though it might have been his father's, threatening smacks if Ham and Shem weren't in bed by nine o'clock. There was real imaginative absorption: men fell off the Ark and were rescued, the sons went for an evening swim each night, and Ham pushed a hypodermic needle with a sedative in it into the more ferocious of the animals to calm them down for the night. This last improvisation, incidentally, recalled an episode from the television programme, 'Daktari'.

So, as a framework for improvisation we used basic situations such as the Noah or the train journey to the seaside, or an imaginary environment—'atmosphere based' improvisations as one student called them. For these, we used sound and redeployed the classroom furniture, and we can imagine that where this is possible lighting could also be a means of stimulating imaginative play. For example, we did a fairground and a circus. For the fairground we made a tape with fairground sounds on it—a hurdy-gurdy, people shouting, etc., and the whole class talked about which side-show they were going to play in. There was a coconut shy, a hall of mirrors, a roundabout, a ghost train and a hot-dog stall. Although the play was a bit chaotic, the following week we were bombarded with paintings, poems and stories that had 'come out of it' in one way and another, and this seemed proof enough to us of the efficacy and value of it.

During these afternoon sessions we were able to pay a certain amount of attention to individual children, especially by way of encouraging and bringing out those who were bewildered or timid in the early stages. We noticed how certain children took on their roles with increasing assurance as time went by. Unfortunately, I have not the space here to describe the play of individual children, but I must say something about Harold who baffled and, indeed, deceived us all. To all intents and purposes Harold, a big boy physically, was an anarchic Bully Bottom. He wanted to play all the parts and provide all the sound effects. Unrestrained, Harold reduced every play to an amorphous fracas, and if things were going well he wanted to change to something else. We recognized that his boisterousness contributed *something* to the proceedings, but in our tireder and less charitable moments we felt that Harold was a child we could well do without. We used to conclude our afternoons with somebody telling or reading a twenty-minute story, and it was usually difficult to get started as Harold wanted to fight all and sundry for the place at the reader's right hand, looking over his shoulder at the pictures. From this position he would give the class advanced information on what was coming. On the last afternoon but one, Harold took up a place on the periphery of the class while I read the story, and there he absorbed himself in the drawing of a fierce, colourful, and intricate dragon, the origins of which we never discovered. At the end of the afternoon, Harold handed his dragon to Tony Jones (the other tutor present) who felt and expressed pleasure, and handed it back. 'No, keep it,' said Harold, 'it's a present.' On our last afternoon we rehearsed and performed an impromptu version of the Mummers' play (we were getting quite close to Christmas). Harold seemed the perfect choice for the Turkish Knight and was so cast, but to our astonishment, when his turn came in the final performance to enter the arena and do his part, he was in a state of acute distress and quite unable to go through with it. Perhaps he was upset by the casting;

perhaps being called upon for the first time to act a given part before an audience (his usual classmates) had brought to the surface a timid side of his personality that we had never noticed before. (I should add, for the record, that Harold had regained much of his normal vigour by home time.)

An interesting feature of this work was that, as time went on, the children, quite spontaneously, told us more and more about their own games and songs. When we first played them our tapes, they asked if they could record something. They performed these two group songs for us. The first is accompanied by a rhythmic and intricate hand-clapping pattern, in which the singers clap, in turn, their own and their neighbours' hands:

Under the blankets, under the sheets
Bom bom bom bom
True love for ever, true love for me
And when we're married we'll raise a family
Under the blankets, under the sheets
Bom bom bom bom

The second song is punctuated by appropriate mime and imitative sound:

When Susie was a baby
A baby Susie was
And she went
  (baby cries)

When Susie was a'christened etc.
When Susie was a child etc.
When Susie was a teenager etc.
When Susie was a'courting etc.
When Susie was a'married etc.
When Susie was a mother etc.
When Susie was a'drowning etc.
When Susie was a'dying etc.
When Susie was a'dead etc.
When Susie was in heaven etc.

When Susie was a ghost etc.
When Susie was an angel etc.

We were delighted (and not a little shaken) by these playground pieces, and although we did not follow them up in our classroom drama, they were interesting to us because they seemed to reflect qualities that were present in the more convincing and coherent passages of the children's drama. Both the songs and the drama express a preoccupation with fundamental life/play roles, and functions such as eating and being eaten, exercising authority and reacting to it, dressing, sleeping, intruding and repelling intruders, death and rebirth, cultivating one's own patch, and so on. Expression of these preoccupations tends to be direct, extroverted and conventional, and, from time to time, to take on a strong controlling form and rhythm, often reflecting the forms of traditional folk verse and story.

The language of these Tuesday afternoons—which were filled with active gossip, story and drama—was predominantly expressive, and constantly pressing towards a poetic mode as the children's experience found symbolic forms, and the images of fiction were worked on in terms of their own experience. As teachers we welcomed those moments when the children's experience took on the shape, coherence and clarity of sustained pieces of narrative, mime, dialogue, and the writing and painting that was done in between our visits. At another extreme, the children's expressiveness occasionally seemed to some of us disturbingly like rowdyism: movement, talk, and even listening, were a competition for the limelight, acts of aggression against the group. Yet it would be wrong to feel that these Tuesday afternoon activities were valuable only at those times when children's expression found a poetic, or near poetic, shape, for, whereas work at this more *formal* level had about it a ritual simplicity like that of the playground songs and games, it was, for the most part, in the *informal* interactions that children discovered what they had to say, reflected, qualified, and expressed explicit personal judgements.

The play/drama of these children, with its accompanying song, story, painting, writing, gives a hint of the way that a class of children, with their teacher, might create their own culture—an organic culture rather than an imposed system—a society in which the individual can discover his identity and learn to live with other people. A full and colourful description of such a process in another context is to be found in Elwyn Richardson's book, *In the Early World* (New Zealand Foundation for Educational Research).

A good deal of children's work in drama will come out of themselves, out of their own first-hand experience of life. There is a sense in which their encounter with stories is dramatic: they act out the events of the story in the theatre of their own imaginations, and, adopting one role or another (perhaps one role after another) from the story, they involve themselves in the events. Margaret Spencer's article offers insights into some of the ways in which children engage with stories as revealed in their written reports of them. We see in her examples the shift in perspective and demands of language that take place in moving from the direct 'being' of drama to the 'writing about' of report. Mr. Burton sees drama as a matter of 'doing' and 'being' rather than 'performing': Mrs. Spencer's account of children reporting on stories prompts us to suggest that it might often be more profitable to ask children to *'tell us about* the play you have been making up' rather than *'show* us your play'.

STORIES AND STORYTELLING

Margaret Spencer

The core of this article is work done by Ralph Lavender at De Lucy School with second and fourth year junior children. His concern was to relate certain story books the children were reading to 'topic' work in other subject areas and to see what, if anything, came back from the stories in other forms and how the children used the reading and telling of stories.

What a deal of anxiety we should be rid of if we knew exactly what children's reading did for them and to them. If only we were sure that literary diet could be calculated as if it were calories and vitamins so that we might confidently prescribe for deficiencies, allow for overweight and calculate growth in terms of personality. But all we know for certain is that we do *not* know which book will win over which child to become a reader instead of a print-gasper, and despite all the surveys which go on continuously of what children read, we are still largely in the dark about the real difference books make. Perhaps we can answer the question only about ourselves, and then something which seems largely irrelevant to the fact of literature may loom large; an asthmatic eight-year-old has more time to read than his more active peers and the myopic teenager is rarely in the first eleven for either games or glamour. In both cases we might be disposed to say that reading was 'making up' for what was missed elsewhere.

But reading habits are sufficiently predictable, or commonly conditioned, for publishers to advance sums of money for mss which fall into the categories of 'family stories', 'boys' adventure 8-10', 'historical fiction' and for authors to accept these and still produce distinctive books. The children's editors, concerned at least as much with the product as the profits, say that a good plot is absolutely necessary because they know that the need to be told a story, with or without a book, is a constant factor in the life of children at home and at school. In Mr. Britton's words story telling seems to offer the child the chance of 'testing out to the limits the possibilities of experience'. What we want to know more precisely is how this happens.

In the early stages each child experiences the spectator role in a particular way with regard to stories, and the quality of this experience, the warmth of human contact in being read to, the shock of recognition in hearing what other people do, the magic of being transported to other times and places, seems to influence the way in which they later come to regard literature. We say 'seems' because the testimony comes mostly from devoted and persistent readers. In the classroom children first meet stories as a spell-binding exercise when the teacher reads and they sit and listen quietly. For some children this may be their first live social contact with a storyteller, although they would regard T.V. as offering the same thing. For all the calm, their listening is intensely active. They may break into the narrative with 'My dad's got a barrow like that' or 'We grow turnips on an allotment' even when the story is something magical or a poem by Lewis Carroll. This 'latching in' through what they know seems to suggest their moving into the spectator role. While it is difficult for the teacher to tolerate too many interruptions in the flow of the narrative, the child needs the assurance that his experience is relevant, and his contributions help him to develop in this role. In the discussions which may, but not necessarily must, follow, other contributions will be received and exchanged.

Later, even many days later, we may find the substance of a story coming into the children's play, sometimes in a form we do not immediately recognize. The Frog Prince at tea in the Wendy house is easy to spot, the little girl scolding a little boy as 'Bad Harry' in the language of *My Naughty Little Sister* is more puzzling if the boy's name is John and he has done nothing naughty. By the time children are six we see that they need stories, as they need all kinds of other things, as an earnest of their growing up, because in listening or reading they transcend the limitations of their state. Stories of naughty children allow them to meditate on their own naughtiness; magic, as Roger Lancelyn Green says[1], is just out of their reach. They use it to extend their play and their games and they make stories their own with the whole of themselves in a way they rarely do again.

Spell-binding is not the teacher's prerogative. Story telling goes on officially and unofficially all day long between teacher and taught, mostly in the form of anecdotes. Children quickly learn that marvels get a hearing and that there is something about the way a story is told that makes a difference. You hear them experimenting with this as they tell each other jokes. These are important because they are short enough to keep an important listener (*he* has one to tell) attentive to the end, the sting in the tail guarantees a good raconteur an audience reaction, and the fun often lies in an experiment with language:

> An' there was this man with 'is new car, an' he
> asked a lady to come with 'im in 'is new car,
> an' she was French and she didn't speak English
> so he said, will you come with me in my new
> car, an' she said, 'Wee wee' an' he said, no you
> won't, not in my new car.

Amongst the multiplicity of satisfactions the *form* is patently one.

Alongside the continuous exchange of ancedote and the use of story material for the children's own purposes there is a special ritual connected with 'the story' being read in the classroom; it is one of the most significant times in all teaching and we should promote it to make the most of the quality of the listening, that group-generated enchantment. The stories we read embody our beliefs about literature. We know from the increased interest in and criticism of imaginative fiction for children that children's books differ from adult books in degree rather than in kind, that good authors of books for children are informed by the same concerns as writers of adult literature but they take the matter of childhood as their theme. Thus, while it may be right and proper to let children exercise a deal of choice in what they read for themselves, books chosen for them by the teacher transmit the teacher's literary judgment. Also, in selecting what to read, the teacher contributes developmentally to the children's experience. Some stories do no more than bring about 'the effortless recognition of what is reasonably and comfortably familiar',[2] while others offer a vital, active encounter which extends the child so that he enters into the narrative *as if he were* part of it, *and at the same time* could talk to the author.

Children know what it is to be carried away by a tale, then they ask that most important question: 'Is it true?' When this happens we tend to assume they are saying 'Could this really happen and if so could it happen to me?' Our assumption may be right, but it is also true, as Tolkien says, that children are capable of ' "*literary belief*" when the storyteller's art is good enough to produce it'; so that the question 'is it true?' proceeds 'from the child's desire to know what kind of literature he is faced with'. He is, in fact, separating in his own mind stories from life. This is his definition, to himself, of his role as spectator.

The largest number of stories we consider most suitable for younger children come from collections of folk tales and fairy tales. From studies such as Tolkien's[3] and Elizabeth Cook's[4] we better understand the archetypal nature of this literary experience, its relationship to children's fantasies and children's developmental need to relate and to separate the inner and outer realities of experience. When children write fairy stories of their own they recapture the strength of the emotional content in the straightforwardness of the telling[5]:

> The king lived in a palace. Two tall, thin ladies looked after him. The king had bricks but every time he built castles with them they fell down. The two tall thin ladies fed the king on sausages and chips, treacle tart and ice cream. He also had a car with a flag, but he was lonely, he had noone to play with. One day near the castle he saw a house with red shutters and a red roof. Out came a little girl called Rose. The king said, 'I will play with you.' They played hide-and-seek and 'he' all

day. When he went home the two tall thin ladies scolded the king. 'Rose has no crown,' they said, 'We will find a real princess with golden hair and a crown, you will play with her.' The king was sad because the only playmate he wanted was Rose. 'I know,' said the king, 'I will take my crown off and then I can play with anyone I like.' But when he went to play with Rose a little boy came out. He said his name was David. He said, 'What do you want?'

'I want to know where Rose is,' said the king.

'She has moved.'

'Alas!' said the king, 'My one and only playmate has gone.' A few weeks later, somebody bought the king's palace. Now Rose lived in a block of flats. And while the king was looking for a palace he had to stay there. When he found Rose he was so pleased that he decided to stay with her.[5]

Victoria
6 years

This child's literary precedents are a mixture of fairy tale and the newer picture books. Already she distinguishes the language she deems appropriate ('Alas, said the king') and joins her everyday life to her story appreciation, rounding it off with the assurance of the Jacobs versions of old folk tales.[6]

The best fairy stories seem to offer the reader an inner consistency of reality by which he sees his own share of the human dilemma better as the result of a visit to the land of faerie. (Imitation fairy stories offer a milder escapism which is not the same thing.) Moreover, legends are the depositories of wonder and fear, both of which are visible in the children's versions. The closeness of the fairy tales to the oral tradition means that even when he is reading them for himself the child is caught up in the telling. Our evidence confirms that these are the archetypes of literature most readily available *as wholes* to children at this stage and the nearer other books written for them aspire to this condition (adventure, daring, heroism, fantasy), the more readily they are accepted.

In reading the heroic tales the children pick out the author's admiration for the hero's strength. In many of the pieces we collected we can see the children responding to the feeling tone which carries over into other battle pieces as are found in tales of chivalry and episodes in history such as the Crusades. It comes over in the directness of the children's versions:

> Black Hawk was wrestling with the demon. The Demon's Talons scratched Black Hawk's back. After a long fight Black Hawk got hold of the Demon and wrung its neck.
> He took the Birds that he had killed back to the village. When the chief saw Black Hawk with the birds in his hand he said to his tribe 'Black Hawk is a brave man. He will be chief of our tribe when I die.' That's made Black Hawk a Hero.

Amongst their other great virtues, folk tales, legends and heroic tales offer children the chance to understand the nature of the spectator activity by giving them certain conventions within which to contain experience and look at it. Victoria's story certainly does this. Here is another example. The Theseus story was read in class and talked about. Given a chance to write anything she liked this child made a version for herself to keep. See how explicit she is [5]:

> Theseus, the son of King Aegeus was setting sail to go to the island of Crete to kill the fearful monster, the Minotaur. Theseus was going with seven young women and six young men who were all going to be given to the Minotaur to be eaten. When they reached Crete Theseus told them to stand at the entrance of the labyrinth where the Minotaur lived. Princess Ariadne, daughter of King Minos of Crete, fell in love with Theseus and gave him a ball of wool which he tied to the beginning of the labyrinth to unroll on his way. Theseus went in, saw the sleeping Minotaur, leapt upon

him and with a swing of his sword cut off his head. Then, re-winding the wool, he found his way back to his companions full of victory. In all his excitement he forgot to change the sails of the ship. He had promised to sail back with the white sails if he had killed the Minotaur. When Theseus sailed back with the black sails, the poor king dived into the sea and was drowned.

Nicola
8 years

Besides its special place in the classroom as 'the story', narrative has its uses in the extension and illustration of topic work. There is every reason why a good and varied selection of stories should be linked to the more factual material, especially when, as in the case of historical fiction, the author's appeal to the reader's imagination is the strongest reinforcement of the teacher's concern to interest the children. With this in mind, Ralph Lavender set about collecting from the second- and fourth-year juniors examples of writing which bore directly on stories which had been read in class. We then postulated certain categories of response, that is, ways by which we might trace the original story in the child's own narrative or written work. Were we to do it again we should greatly extend both the number and the kind of stories used and the range of the writing. From the material we collected it is clear that, despite the excellence of some examples, children write their best stories when they are unconcerned with some other narrative. Their best stories are their own, when the literary models have been most completely assimilated. However, we have some significant examples in our collection of the traces left by expert story-telling, enough to let us know what is happening.

Among the books used, not all of which were read to or by all the children, were Macaulay's *Lay of Horatius*, *The Eagle of the Ninth*, *Knight Crusader*, *Knight's Fee*, fables of Aesop, stories of Robin Hood, highwayman stories, *Elidor*, *The Hound of Ulster*, *Flood*

Warning, Speed Six, legends of Perseus, Daedalus, etc., *Bobby Brewster, The King of the Golden River*—a good and varied selection.[7]

The first and clearest result is that in retelling stories they have read or heard the children take on the viewpoint of the author and identify themselves with the chief character as if they had created him. But they also assume that the listener or the reader knows as much as they do, how the story goes on, how it ends. There is an almost Biblical undifferentiation of characters, which in its way is quite clear:

> There is this man and he ...
> He set off on a lonely night one the wet roads and
> lightning flashing and pouring with rain then a
> stage coach come passed they heard the sound
> of galloping hooves. But he was ready waiting in
> a bush for them and then they came softly
> trotting parst. But then he said stand and deliver
> and the people in the stage coach were terfied and
> they were screaming....

The total immersion of the teller results in a version which has great sweep and power. It drives on, if somewhat confusedly for the over-sophisticated reader. Compare that with the older child's attempts to retell a story so that the characters and actions are clearly differentiated for the reader:

> Romulus was the first ruler of Rome, and when
> he died a man named Tarquin ruled, but he was
> very cruel and wicked so a man named Mucius
> and a lot of the people sent Tarquin and his
> family out of Rome. But a man called Lars Porsena
> a friend of Tarquin wanted to get him back, and
> he got two other men that were on his side, which
> realy sons of Mucius....

As the child's egocentrism declines, so he begins to put the reader in full possession of the facts of the tale, and the narrative flood decreases. His growth in awareness of what is involved in storytelling sometimes means a loss of immediacy. To account for the strict chronology in most accounts of this kind Marjorie Hourd suggests that 'the fear of being at the mercy of the irrational parts of the personality' is 'one of the reasons why it is difficult to forsake the chronological in writing'.[8] Also children believe that a story has a certain kind of accepted pattern and do their best to be faithful to it.

We next looked for the developmental advance in children's thinking and storytelling which comes with the introduction of the notion of consequence in narrative, but found again that juxtaposition of events is still the child's main way of handling them.[9] The consequential incidents are recalled separately without connection:

> That night a group of boys dicided to sail out to get help. They sailed over to an old mill. The boys climbed up the mill. *But* one boy fell in. *When the boys left the mill* they sailed away and had only sardines for lunch. (*Flood Warning.*)

A crucial link is missing but to the reader the important point is not the relationship of one event to the next, but the ongoingness of the story. What happens to the boy who fell in does not seem of first importance at this stage. Although the children understand the nature of the sequence of events, in this kind of writing they expect the reader to supply the causal relationships, whereas in stories they write for themselves they begin with *motive*. Here the details are more important:

> All the parts were checked. Tyres engeen etc. they were at the starting line and there off after about two hours Johnny wild crashed on a path (? patch) of oil he was not very bad. Just dazed and the diane was badly smashed up when Johnny wild woke up in hospital danny Black said your going to be all right. (*Speed Six.*)

Where the writer is not concerned to report consequence

he/she has little awareness of incongruity. One child begins a story by explaining how his hero had been 'crippled for life' at a time when this would have meant immobility. He sees no reason why he should not continue 'When he was walking down the street he met his sister-in-law'. As Piaget says, 'Childish logic is lacking in necessity.'

The syncretistic nature of some children's narrative shows us that once they are involved in the role of story-teller or of reader they find it difficult to extricate themselves to report on the story itself. Yet teachers ask pupils quite early on in their school career to tell them about the stories, to act as judges of their own and other people's. Not content with asking them if they like a story, or, as in the earlier stages, looking for a later effect in their play, teachers tend to expect verbal rejoinders to match their own and are sometimes disappointed when a reader who has been so patently absorbed, has little to say about the story:

> I think the book called *Elidor* was quite esciting because at the beginning it sounded like some children playing but in the middle it is very scaring. At the end it is very sad because a unicorn died.

But there is a great deal of feeling tone which is more significant than what is actually said. Where there is no intention to review a book in terms suggested by the teacher, judgment is rarely included in the account given of the story. Descriptions are pictorial reconstructions rather than assessments.[1]

> I thought the story of Bobby Brewster was very good. I liked the way Mr. Todd fitted his words in. The part of the story where the bottom of the dustbin came out and where the Long Dustman who was six foot tall came up and knocked the dustbin against a van and left a Dent at the side of the dustbin. I have a new dustbin at home

and already it has a dent in it where the dustman
has banged the side on the lorry and dented it.

Here there is no detachment from the happening in order
to judge the telling. Instead the enjoyment is enhanced
because it confirms an experience which already has some
significance.

Puffin Post, which has regular examples of children's
reviewing, confirms this notion in each issue, while occasionally trying to prod even the most bookish young
into saying more about 'the characters and the setting';
but ten- and eleven-year-olds still need to do the job
for themselves rather than to please a teacher or even
a very sympathetic and insightful editor[10]:

> I AM DAVID by Anne Holm
> David was born in a concentration camp, and
> lived there until he was twelve. A man (whom
> David hated) helped David to escape. He knew
> nothing about the outside world, what to eat,
> and so on.
> David, determined to live, made a dangerous and
> frightening journey through the perilous winds
> and weather. On his way to Denmark, he met many
> people who threatened to hand him over to the
> Police, who would probably give David to 'them'.
> Eventually David reached Denmark where he met
> his mother.
> There aren't any pictures in this book but it is
> so well described that I could imagine things in
> my own mind.
>
> Susan Lisser
> 11 years old

In the retelling the tone is significant and sometimes the
skill in handling the plot details is an indication that the
reader is feeling his way into the author's role as spectator. The children's author is sympathetic to this, hence
the excellence of plot construction in children's books
and the organic fusion of character, dialogue and action
in the best of them.

It would seem important, therefore, not to rely on reviews to assess children's responses and development. Far better is an awareness of general atmosphere in which books and stories are regularly discussed, exchanged, read aloud, acted and linked to other work. Here is another example from *Puffin Post*[11]:

> We'd all heard about Vikings, but last year we read in class THE HORNED HELMET by Henry Treece, and then we made a play about the raid.
> It was very exciting. We felt just like the Vikings, and some of the boys seemed to go berserk. Later we wrote some poems, these were two of them (of which we print one—editors):

The Horned Helmet

> The vikings did not care a hang.
> They approached. Barbaric gang.
> I stayed in my hut.
> They broke in. They treasure took.
> People killed, people taken.
> Over the sea the Vikings come,
> Murdering, burning, stealing, plundering,
> Attack by night or by day,
> The Vikings come.
> They plunder in the west, north, south, east.
> Their ships are made for iron.
> With their swords they take the treasure
> Of the begotten sun.

The crucial point is 'we felt like the Vikings' and that feeling meant trying out words like 'berserk', 'slaken', 'begotten', and making strong short lines, to push the experience further. He might even conclude that the best judgments are those which are made in the reproduction of the tone of the original in retelling the plot or in making a wholly new thing: e.g. a poem, a different story.

This may also emerge in a later concern with form, reminiscent of the earlier joke, where the audience is now wider. To examine this, we looked at children's responses to fables and asked them to write one.

The Giraffe Who Wanted a Short Neck

There was once a giraffe who loved honey. He had found a broken jar once and had licked the contents out. The giraffe knew that honey came from bees and he also knew that there happened to be some bees in a hollow tree. The only trouble was the hole was low down in the tree and the giraffe had not got enough space to spread his legs out and bend down because he was in a forest. 'If I had a shorter neck I would just have to lick the honey out,' said the giraffe. The giraffe was rather a stupid one and he thought that if he had banged his head against a tree his neck would get shorter. The result was he only made himself dizzy. There was a sprite in the wood who said he would give the giraffe a short neck for a day. The giraffe was ever so pleased, until lunch time. He could not reach his favourite leaves, nor could he reach the grass. He tried to get the honey, but only got stung. He asked the sprite if he could have his neck back and the sprite said yes.
Motto: BE SATISFIED WITH WHAT YOU HAVE GOT! (Written by an above average 11 year old after reading fables.)

We have no evidence of the growth of this kind of awareness (although Piaget shows that we could probably have looked for it[12]) because we did not deliberately set out to collect it, but the fable is a sophisticated development despite the apparent simplicity of the material and this effort shows what the penetrative enjoyment of the *form* can produce. The enthusiasm for the *double entendre* helps the idea of the literary form, and the very formality promotes the appreciation of the narrative.

Awareness of form in storytelling shows itself in the writer's need to complete what he is retelling, however wrenched or arbitrarily rounded off. The completion has a ring of necessity. 'And that was the last robbery'. 'Most of the engered (injured) people have recovered'. One can also see him beginning to wrestle with the balance of detail and climax. The younger children spend longer on the initial details then rush to the end; the older ones begin to spread the load. Possibly the evidence we have for the reader's concentration on the climax shows the teacher's selection rather than what the children find memorable. This is about *The Eagle of the Ninth*, the crux of the story in fact, and most remarkable, as it shows a grasp of the crucial point.

The Eagle of the Ninth

Marcus was a Romen sentren he was badly hert *so he had to go** to Scotland. They met a man named Guern. One night Marcus noticed that Guern had a mark on his face of a Romen helmet. He said 'why have you got the mark of a Romen helmet'. Then Guern said 'I was in the ninth legion. Most of us was dead of ill and the villeges started on us and captured the Eagle and took it round the villeges and most of us went and sarted to live like them.' Then Marcus said 'do you know where my father is he has the eagle holder.' Guern said 'I have now ider where he is he must of gine to live in a villeg'. 'Why don't you come back to the fort with us said Marcus. Guern said no I could not. Besides I have a wife and son. I could not lave them. All right said Marcus. In the mornig they set out to get the Eaget.
(Written by a below average 11 year old after parts of *The Eagle of the Ninth* had been read to the class.)

The selection of detail is nowhere more significant than in the historical novel. Publishers tend to avoid producing full-blown books of this kind (such as those of Cynthia Harnett, Rosemary Sutcliff, Ronald Welch) for children under ten because they believe that the subtleties

---

* Her notion of consequence is wrong.

of historical events are beyond children of this age. But as historical novels have some of the best stories available at present, the under 12's respond to these, as far as they can, and find the details memorable. It is by these very details that the historical feeling is conveyed. For example, during a topic on The Crusades an able fourth-year boy wrote:

Crusader Life

'William, get my hauberk for me will you' said Sir John de Corenian, to his best squire William, 'Tomorrow I have to see Richard the Lion Heart and I will go in my full fighting dress, so I want it polished to perfecsion, so boy don't just stand there, get on with it!' William went to his room and started to polish. Later he returned with the armour, highly polished, and gave it to Sir John 'Here you are Sir, I hope you like the polishing', 'very well done indeed, you may go to the city if you like now.' *He walked across the soft Turkish carpet to his room. The room had a large tapestrie on the wall, and the room was dull because of the silk curtains covering the windows.* He drew them aside. He could see the city of Jerusalem, *the temple of the rock's dome glinted in the hot holy land sun.* 'I think I will go to the city now' said William and he went down to the stables to get a horse. He mounted and rode away. He arrived in the city about ½ an hour later. He went to the old market place to see what he could buy. Lady Freda had asked him to get her a new tapestrie, so he bought one and went to look around, after 2 hours, in the city he rode home into the setting sun.

Into the form of a similar piece a girl of ten has poured much of her longing:

The quintain stood lifeless in the middle of the courtyard. Jo the cooks girl (the image of a boy) stood at one end of the courtyard stroking Jamier

145

the tilting horse. Jo and Jamier were very good friends. All of a sudden she put down her boull (she was peeling onions) and backed Jamier out of the stable. She was going to get a belting for being late but what did she care. She put a blanket onto Jamier's back, took up a lance and climbed onto Jamier's back. All at once she found herself (unwillingly) charging at the quintain she imagined crowds of people shouting for her and in her dreams she saw King John himself calling for her to win. Bang! she hit the quintain 'Wait wait' called a voice 'your just the boy I need' for you remember she looked like a boy. This man (who Jo was soon to lern was Mr. Poffliffe) signed Jo up for a jousting compition that afternoon King John would be there. So Jo appeared at a jousting compition (with Jamier) and won and King John presented Jo with her prize which was a white linin sercoat. She didn't have to imangaing any more for this was the real thing.

This passage shows how children write under the influence of what they read and is the more important for that because it seems to be written from the inside, from the totality of the response to this kind of reading whereby the strange words and ideas (quintain, jousting, sur-coat) become part of the reader's whole experience.

These results may be special rather than typical. In examining the language the children use, as in these examples, we are perhaps safe in guessing at a literary origin. We can be fairly sure, however, that some things would not have been said unless they had antecedent forms of the same kind in story telling or reading.

In the pieces by the younger children one is struck by the immediacy of the dialogue. In the books they read most of the action is carried by the dialogue:

Cuchulain went up to the Princess Aifa and said: 'Let us carry out the battle. Princess Aifa was willing and said 'yes'.

We see them trying out word patterns:

> Down and down the canal she went ...
> It was so nice, it had tulips in a baby's pen
> and it looked rather grand....
> Suddenly the grappling irons were hitting the
> side, then the boarding party swarmed over on to
> the enemy's ship.

> The bell for break. Every corridor was full of
> babbling squelling children. Vicomte Hubert raced
> to the porch for his father's blue jag. It never
> did appear.

The most impressive is the children's response to situations involving formality or ritual. The language assumes a hieratic quality which is certainly literary in origin. It has stateliness and dignity and shows well the readers' sense of occasion:

> At this Cuchulain put his dagger to her neck and
> he pulled her war cap off her head and seeing that
> she was so beautiful he dared not kill her....

They mix the formal with the everyday:

> 'Thank you kindly, sire', said the knight.
> 'That's all right', said Robin Hood. 'By the way,
> I do not no your name.'

Or they pour the matter of their play into the legend outline in the way most teachers recognize and of which most classrooms provide examples:

The Hold Up

> The scene is set in Sherwood Forest. The wood is
> thick on either side of the road.
> Characters: Robin Hood
>   Little John
>   1st Outlaw

2nd Outlaw
Bishop
Priest

Robin: Here comes the priest and Bishop, they have probably got the taxes. Quick! hide in the bushes.

Little John: Do you think they saw us?

Robin: I don't think so.

1st Outlaw: They are getting close Robin, shall we jump them.

Robin: Yes, come on lads.

Bishop: What is the meaning of this?

Robin: We are here to take the taxes, to give back to the poor people.

Priest: If you take the money the Sheriff of Nottingham shall hear of it.

2nd Outlaw: Come on hurry up and tell us where it is.

Bishop: In the bag.

Robin: Will, go and get it.

Will: (Walking over to the horse) Alright, Robin.

Bishop: You won't get away with this.

Robin: We'll see about that. Have you got it Will?

W.2nd O: Yes.

Robin: Come on let's go (Walking off).

Priest: Come back you outlaws.

Robin: (Shouting) We will when you have more taxes.

(Written by an average girl from the East End of London after talking about stories of Robin Hood.)

Although we have by no means categorized all the significant forms of story-telling by children, we are most conscious of the amount of solid enjoyment which comes across from this written work. When we are concerned to know what difference story telling has made to their lives we have to think of all the penetrative insight which the quoted pieces reveal, the kind of living which these books seem to offer.

At the same time we are bound to see that we might easily underrate the power of narrative and expressive language in topic work, both in the books we read to the children and in the books they read to further their own interests. We may be too concerned to intervene between the story and the child with questions about the content or his understanding, when we could instead give him more opportunities to express his response in other forms.

We may not have done justice to all the children's efforts to provide us with material to show storytelling as a typical classroom activity, but that is not the fault of the children. It is pretty clear that, as they do in writing, so do we in reading what they write, draw a little nearer to the truth about ourselves.

References

1 Green, R. L., 'The Golden Age of Children's Books', in *Essays and Studies*, English Association, (J. Murray, 1962)

2 Rosenheim, E. W. Jr., *Children's Reading and Adult Values*, The Library Quarterly, (University of Chicago Press, 1967)

3 Tolkien, J. R. R., *Tree and Leaf*, (Allen and Unwin, 1964)

4 Cook, Elizabeth, *The Ordinary and the Fabulous*, (C.U.P., 1969)

5 From a collection of writing by children at Redcliffe School, London

6 Jacobs, Joseph, *English Folk Tales*, (Bodley Head, 1968)

7 See below to list of children's books

8 Hourd, M. and Cooper, G. E., *Coming into Their Own*, (Heinemann, 1959)

9 Piaget, Jean, *Judgement and Reasoning in the Child*, (Routledge, 1928)

10 Webb, Kaye, (ed.), *Puffin Post*, vol. 4, No. 1, (Penguin, 1970)

11 Ibid., vol. 1, No. 1, (Penguin, 1967)

12 Piaget, J., *Language and Thought of the Child*, (Routledge, 1959)

Books for children mentioned in the text

Additional Bibliography

Egoff, S., Egoff, G. T. and Ashley, L. F., *Only Connect: readings on Children's literature*, (O.U.P., 1970)
Fenwick, S. I., (Ed.), *A Critical Approach to Children's Literature*, (University of Chicago Press, 1967)

Berna, Paul, *Flood Warning*, (Bodley Head)
Carter, Bruce, *Speed Six*, (Longmans and Puffin)
Edwards, Dorothy, *My Naughty Little Sister*, (Faber)
Garner, Alan, *Elidor*, (Collins and Puffin)
Sutcliff, Rosemary, *The Eagle of the Ninth*, (O.U.P.)
—— *Knights Fee*, (O.U.P.)
—— *The Hound of Ulster*, (Bodley Head)
Todd, H., *Bobby Brewster*, (Brockhampton)

In his bibliography, Professor Britton cites D. W. Harding's article in *Scrutiny*, 'The Role of the Onlooker', as seminal to some of his own thinking (in particular, his spectator/participant distinction). Professor Harding briefly restates and then develops ideas from this article in 'Psychological Processes in the Reading of Fiction' (*British Journal of Aesthetics*, 1962—reprinted in *Aesthetics and the Modern World*, edited by Harold Osborne (Thames and Hudson, 1968)). Thus he writes:

> ... I agree with those who maintain that the numerous and extremely dissimilar activities conventionally grouped together as the arts don't form a separate psychological category. Very few literal statements that apply to a novel, a landscape painting, a porcelain dish and a piece of music will be at all illuminating about any one of those things. A novel is so distantly related to many other sorts of art, and so closely related to activities that are not included among the arts, that an approach through aesthetic generalizations would be restricting and misleading. It may seem, perhaps, that the form of a novel and the style of a novelist can be discussed in terms equally applicable to other arts, but I suspect that it can be done only by substituting metaphor and analogy for literal statement.
>
> Much more important aspects of fiction are illuminated if the reader of a novel is compared with the man who hears about other people and their doings in the course of ordinary gossip. And to give an account of gossip we have to go a step or two farther back and consider the position of the person who looks on at actual events ...

Later, Professor Harding goes on, for instance, to make important criticisms of 'pseudo-psychologizing that sees the process of novel-reading as one of identification and vicarious experience'. He deals with this and related matters, in a more easily accessible form, in 'Considered Experience' (*English in Education*, vol. 1, No. 2, N.A.T.E. & O.U.P., Summer 1967).

Most of the books mentioned on page 53 in connection with children's writing concern themselves with literature, both poetry and fiction. In addition, the reader should find helpful matter in the following: *Young Writers, Young Readers* edited by Boris Ford (Hutchinson) (for example, Douglas Brown's article on Stevenson in which he tackles, in a way that has general implications, the question of the most appropriate age for children to read *Treasure Island* and *Kidnapped*); *I Could a Tale Unfold: Violence, Horror and Sensationalism in Stories for Children* by P. M. Pickard (Tavistock) and *Children and Stories* by Anthony Jones and June Buttrey (Blackwell) (whose preoccupations are related to Professor Britton's: the book begins—'Stories are not books . . .'). Although Margery Fisher's *Intent upon Reading* (Brockhampton) is not as discriminating as it might have been to some purpose, it remains an indispensable survey. The most useful chapters of Marie Peel's *Seeing to the Heart: English and Imagination in the Junior School* (Chatto and Windus) are perhaps those on 'Story' and 'Projects': they contain a wealth of suggestions, amounting almost to a survey from a pedagogical point of view. Vol. 5, No. 3 (Autumn 1970), of *English in Education* is devoted to *Reading* broadly defined.

The writers so far in this book have concerned themselves very little with what preoccupies many parents and teachers: spelling, etc. However, this does not mean that they think the conventions should be ignored. The following article aims to recognize their place—but also to put them in it.

||||||||||||||||||||||||||||||||||||||||||||||||||||||||||||||||||||||||||||||||||||||||||||||||||

SPELLING, ETC.

Nancy Martin and Jeremy Mulford

Teachers commonly talk about the 'basic skills', especially in connection with reading, writing and arithmetic. The phrase itself provides the explanation for this. First, any concern with what is of lasting value seems to imply a need for solid foundation, a basis. Secondly, 'skill' has the attraction for a teacher of seeming to be something which can not only be objectively defined but also exist in its own right and *therefore* be passed on as a sort of entity. Because of this, it is not surprising that the notion of 'skill' is often translated into the image of a 'tool'. Now a tool in the literal sense is useless without the competence to use it. But 'tool' in the figurative sense incorporates that competence; and so it reassuringly obscures the fact that, in the case of writing for example, skill cannot be adequately defined merely as something the teacher imparts and which the pupil comes to possess in so far as he is ready to do so. We say 'reassuringly' because this conception puts a considerable onus on the teacher—he is then *in charge* of *what is to be learned*; and usually, the more one is in control of a situation, the more reassured one feels. We would go on to suggest that the teacher who does not question what he means by 'skills' —whose notion of them expresses, or has lurking behind it, a feeling that skills are in some sense entities—will be all the readier to see the conventions (of spelling, punctuation, etc.) as 'basic' to writing. For the conventions are by definition held in common, impersonal, and can be considered in isolation. By an easy extension, competence in using them can also be considered in isolation, and hence as something which the teacher who possesses it can impart to pupils who don't. This, to repeat, is reassuring. But we would maintain that a child who observed all the conventions with perfect competence, yet whose writing was uniformly unengaged, should not be called a skilled writer—not even in a 'basic' sense. Indeed, it would be precisely what is basic that was lacking in his writing behaviour. We use, here, the phrase 'writing behaviour' in order to stress the *activity* of writing, the process, as against the *product*.

Christian Schiller writes in *Talking and Writing**:

> It can be argued that logically reading comes before writing; but there must have been a first writer before there was a reader. Young children like to be such a first writer, putting down, regardless of others, what they want to say. It is not writing in the sense that it is written to be read; often it cannot be read except by the writer. Even if it can be read by others it is not the written word that is read, but a record of speech. John wants to talk about some experience he has enjoyed, and he records what he would say. If his pencil is very slow it helps occasionally to record it for him. Here is such a recording of a boy just seven, who lived in the country.

>> One day in autumn I went for a walk in a wood, and in a tree I saw a nest. I thought it was rather strange to see a nest in autumn, especially when a bird flew off it. I wondered what bird's nest it was. I thought it was a hooded crow's nest, but I knew it couldn't be in the part of England where I lived. I wanted to try and climb the tree, but the tree was too thin. The colours of the bird that flew from the nest were black and white. I thought it was very strange to see a bird's nest in autumn. I wished I could see inside the nest, but I knew I couldn't because the tree would break. So I came away, and I am still wondering what bird it was in the nest.

> These words were spoken by a human voice; and black marks lying still and silent on a page cannot convey the melody and rhythm of the spoken sounds. But if one is familiar with the way an eager boy of seven will relate an adventure, slow at first with quickening pace as he lives again the event, something of this melody and rhythm can be felt; and it is this melody and rhythm which give to

---

* Edited by James Britton (Methuen).

the words a quality beyond that of sense, a quality of being alive. But there is more than melody and rhythm; these simple words arranged simply have a shape, a beginning, a middle, and an end; and the simple shape is the more eloquent because the end is almost but not quite a repetition of the beginning. Hearing these words in our inner ear we can vicariously share his adventure, what he saw, what he did, what he felt in the wood one day in autumn.

There is no evidence to lead us to think that he spoke, or would write, deliberately in the way he did, or that he strove consciously to give his words a living quality. Doubtless he used language, as for example he would use paint, to say what was in him to say without concern for giving a considered impression. But in fact, however unconsciously his words were chosen and arranged, they give us something living of himself. He is using language, as he uses paint, not merely to say something but to express something of himself. Already he has begun to grasp the discipline of the material he uses.

Set out in printed words, punctuated and spelt in our contemporary convention, the composition looks exemplary. But it was not consciously spoken in sentences; and punctuation and spelling had no part in the creative act. It is not in these conventions that the discipline has been felt, but in *the choice of what to say and how to say it....*

We have quoted at length because we feel the passage is a classic statement and deserves the widest currency. 'The choice of what to say and how to say it' seems to us the basic skill of writing, though perhaps the word 'choice'—implying as it does, out of context, conscious choice—is not a very apt word to apply to the process, particularly in the case of young children. Yet, since all experience is the raw material of writing, there must be, in fact, selection and shaping in words. The process of writing seems to be primarily a matter of keeping the inward eye focussed on whatever bit of experience the writer wants to record or articulate, and letting the flow of words largely look after itself. When the flow stops from time to time, as it inevitably does, the focus of attention may shift to the words, and conscious choice begin to operate. But whatever the exact nature of this process and its possible varieties may be, we believe—as do Professor Britton and Mr. Schiller—that a function of writing prior to communication is self-discovery, the representation of experience to oneself, for one's own satisfaction. With this in mind, it may be helpful to consider briefly the nature and function of various conventions.

One fundamental distinction that must be made is that between the concept expressed in a particular grammatical form and the conventional means of expressing it. For example, an eleven-year-old might have a good practical understanding of conditionality, yet still write, 'If my dad go to the football match on Saturday, he said he take me with him'. Now there might be general agreement that the conceptual knowledge involved in writing this is much more important than the inaccurate rendering of the conventional inflexions; yet teachers commonly act as though this were not so.* Much concern with correct conventional usage is merely a concern with tidiness for its own sake (to which we are not necessarily hostile—it's a question of priorities); and quite often particular notions of tidiness, of acceptable usage, have a class base. 'They ain't got no' is not a middle class usage, and therefore attracts teachers' red pencils. Yet in many working class environments it is the normal, accepted usage; and moreover, nobody for whom it isn't the accepted usage is likely to be in any doubt as to what it means. There is no Natural Law which states that a second negative cancels the first (Chaucer, a court poet, was not being unconventional for *his* time and social group when he used a double negative, for emphasis). For a teacher to unquestioningly impose† *his* accepted

---

* On promoting the use of 'the complex internal organization that language itself provides for representing relation of sequence and hierarchy and consequence' (James Britton), see Nancy Martin's article, 'What are they up to?'.

† The reader who objects to this split infinitive might, relevantly, ask himself why.

usages of this kind on a child may be at once pointless and harmful. Pointless, because it is often far from clear that it is advantageous to an adolescent about to leave school—let alone a primary school child—that he should have acquired arbitrary middle class linguistic habits. Harmful, because such impositions suggest a failure by the teacher to recognize the prior function of writing that we mentioned in the last paragraph, and because they act cumulatively as a threat to a child's sense of identity which he expresses when he employs the linguistic usages of his home environment.

It is, in fact, difficult if not impossible to judge where to draw the line between usages that are conventional only for tidiness's sake and those that have a greater significance. It is probably more helpful to distinguish between those that have chiefly to do with what we shall call 'presentation', and those that are intrinsic to the communication of meaning. Thus, except in the trivial (because so extraordinary) case of a mis-spelling that is actually the spelling of another word which could reasonably fit the given context, incorrect spelling hardly ever affects significantly the communication of meaning. The margin of error has to be very great before decipherment becomes impossible. Even the famous example of 'egog' becomes comprehensible in such a sentence as 'The egog rolled himself into a ball when the dog sniffed his prickles'—and might well remain so even if the rest of the spelling were grossly inaccurate. It is true that a writer (adult as well as child) may choose to write down a word that he thinks he can spell, but which doesn't precisely capture his meaning, just because he cannot spell the right word. But this would have to do with his awareness, or assumption, of what is socially acceptable.* It would be likely that, given only a rudimentary phonic sense, had he made an incompetent stab

---

* The importance of spelling is often assumed to belong to the Natural Order of Things. A symptom of this is the fact that the incorrect spelling of a person's name is commonly regarded as a particular embarrassment. Yet, Sir Walter Rawleigh (sic), for example, was not very eccentric for his time in varying the spelling of his signature according to whim.

at the spelling of the right word, he would still have succeeded in communicating his meaning.

Much punctuation also belongs, essentially, to the category of 'presentation'. The following is taken from John Clare's 'Journey from Essex' (in which he describes his journey back to his home in Helpstone, Northamptonshire, after escaping from a lunatic asylum in Essex):

> ... I have but a slight reccolection of my journey between here & Stilton for I was knocked up & noticed little or nothing—one night I lay in a dyke bottom from the wind & went to sleep half an hour when I suddenly awoke & found my side wet through from the sock in the dyke bottom so I got out & went on—I remember going down a very dark road hung over with trees on both sides very thick which seemed to extend a mile or two I then entered a town & some of the chamber windows had candle lights shining in them—I felt so weary that I forced [sic] to sit down on the ground to rest myself a while & while I sat there a coach that seemed to be heavy laden came rattling up and stopt in the hollow below me & I cannot reccolect its ever passing by me I then got up & pushed onward seeing little to notice for the road very often looked as stupid as myself & I was very often half asleep as I went on the third day I satisfied my hunger by eating the grass by the road side which seemed to taste something like bread I was hungry and eat heartily till I was satisfied & in fact the meal seemed to do me good the next & last day I reccolected that I had some tobacco & my box of lucifers being exhausted I could not light my pipe so I took to chewing tobacco all day & eat the quids when I had done & I was never hungry afterwards—I remember passing through Buckden ...*

In reading this for the first time, one stumbles occasionally; but to understand precisely what is meant is

---

* J. W. and Anne Tibble, *The Prose of John Clare*, pages 248/9, (Routledge).

not at all difficult.* This example indicates an important distinction: there is a fundamental difference between a passage that is grammatically, syntactically, incoherent, and one that is coherent but lacking the usual signs of this which we call 'punctuation *marks*'. A child's ability to construct sentences may be well in advance of his ability (or inclination) to use full-stops, capital letters, etc. Or, to look at the matter in another way: if all the punctuation marks were removed from, say, *Little Dorrit*, the result would not be a bookful of bad prose.

However, the *Little Dorrit* example raises another issue. Although much of the meaning of the book would not be lost if all punctuation marks were excluded from it, there would be a great many places where an ambiguity was thereby left unresolved (and unresolvable†), or an emphasis (and hence a bit of meaning) lost: such omissions could not be subsumed under the category of 'presentation'. There can be no doubt that, when punctuation marks are intrinsic to the communication of meaning in this way, they are performing their most important function. Yet although it is correct to distinguish between the two main functions of punctuation marks—between occasions when the reader can get by without marks and occasions when, strictly speaking, he cannot—it is impor-

---

* It might be said that the lack of punctuation in this passage contributes to the directness of its impact; or alternatively, that the poignancy of it is all the greater because of the biographical implications of the lack of punctuation. These possibilities are a reminder that one cannot treat 'presentation' as either a simple or a completely separate category. We cannot investigate the matter properly here; but its complexity can perhaps be suggested by imagining a text reproduced in a number of different ways: very inaccurately spelt in immaculate hand-writing, perfectly spelt in almost illegible hand-writing, perfectly spelt in decent hand-writing, typewritten on red paper, printed in huge capitals on newsprint, engraved on cloth paper surrounded by printer's flowers, the same only mis-spelt, and so on—the list could be endless, and it is safe to say that the total meanings communicated would be different—sometimes significantly, sometimes not—in each case.

† i.e., unlike three occasions in the Clare passage. There, technically, we cannot be sure whether a stop would properly come before or after 'as I went on the third day', and before or after 'the next & last day'; nor can we be sure whether it was the box of lucifers that was exhausted, or Clare himself. In practice, we are in no doubt.

tant to recognize that, from another point of view, the two functions belong together: both become significant only if one considers the reader *in addition to the writer*. Thus, someone might write, 'Thunder crashed immediately after the horse bolted the stable collapsed', and *he* would know whether he meant that the thunder crashed after the horse bolted, or that the horse bolted after the thunder crashed. This example returns us to the principle that we stated earlier, concerning 'self-discovery' as against 'communication'.

In speech, children learn very early to say things in different ways on different occasions: that is, their speech is increasingly differentiated, and at a time when their writing is relatively undifferentiated. Despite this fact of development, children are often asked to write in ways they are not capable of—impersonal reports, for instance: they are asked to accept someone else's purpose and mode of writing before they have a sufficiently defined sense of themselves to be capable of seeing purposes separate from their own impulses of the moment. Indeed, it is not simply a matter of purposes. A seven-year-old is not much concerned with his reader beyond the fact that the writing is often seen as an 'offering' to someone who is assumed to understand it just because *he* has written it. The child will not usually make any modification in what he writes, as an adult would, in order to communicate what he is saying. In short, he is writing above all for himself. An adult, too, writes primarily for himself on many occasions: the difference is that an adult's satisfaction in his writing typically includes a sense of his reader reading it—a sense of what is required if satisfactory communication is to take place and of the reader's likely responses, both local and total. The pedagogical implication of this is that great tact is necessary in the face of much writing by young children. If a child has still to reach the stage when the notion of a reader reading what he writes is meaningful to him, an explicit concern chiefly with 'communication' (whether in terms of 'purposes' or of 'presentation' or of *failure* to communicate) on the part of the teacher will be essentially incomprehensible to him. It will tend to stem the impulse towards self-discovery through writing; and if this happens, the teacher's concern will commonly be counter-productive even in its own cause. For a young child to put on record what he *wants* to say, to write so that his language closely fits himself, his experience, to his own satisfaction, seems to us to be skilled writing at this stage of his development; and there will be many occasions when it is better to let him *fail to communicate*, or communicate only inefficiently. We are not suggesting, though, that the teacher should merely wait and see.

The business of helping children directly with their writing is a difficult one. They readily interpret instruction as the learning of rules, and we suggest that the basic matter of writing about what concerns you is not readily susceptible to rules: this is the reason that we make a distinction between skilled writing behaviour and the learning of surface competences. When we try to formulate rules for writing such as 'Have a beginning, a middle, and an end' or 'Make a plan before you write' or 'Here is a list of good words and here is a list of bad ones', we are formulating much simpler and cruder versions than are already being operated.* So we suggest that teachers should beware of rules of this sort, and go for indirect aids such as a rich language experience and opportunities to write from a wide variety of situations—opportunities that the children may take up in any way that fits their concerns. Moreover, it is perhaps relevant that sportsmen are reluctant to talk about the procedures that they operate since they think that being conscious of what they are doing prevents them from operating most efficiently. Poetry may be a better teacher of writing to primary school children than analysis. Poetry works indirectly, analysis is direct ('Why is this word a better one to use than that one?'). The following piece of writing came from a class of eight years olds who had been handling and talking and writing about a green iguana in their classroom:

---

* It is worth remembering that children's use of language at all depends on their operating very complex rules which they don't know exist—which are not for them at any analysable level of knowledge.

The iguana has a long tail to curl with
a long tongue to have fun with
a striped tail to sail with.

Janey

We suggest that the boldness and brevity of this (an example of Professor Britton's 'poetic mode') might well be related to the fact that the children had a lot of poetry read to them, so that this *kind* of language was in their experience continually. The point here is that no one indicated its qualities or asked the children to write according to models. They were simply writing out of a rich language experience, of talking and reading.

But what about the conventions: can the learning of *them* be left to the influence of a 'rich language experience'? The short answer is No; though we believe that such experience should be the main teacher, and that, without it, any direct teaching will be a null activity.

Several points need to be made about the timing of this teaching. First, despite the relative unimportance of the conventions, we are in no doubt that it is desirable that children should have a working knowledge of them by the time they leave school. This does not mean, however, that it is—by definition—better if a child is (say) a competent speller at the age of 10 instead of 15. Such forwardness *may* suggest qualities of intelligence and interest which it is pleasing to find in a child, but the achievement itself is of little consequence. A full recognition of this ought to release much pressure on the primary school teacher. And it should enable him more readily to take the second, related point: if a child is not ready for a particular piece of direct teaching, it will do more harm than good to subject him to it. Thirdly, a child is not 'ready' at the same time to learn all the conventions: we need to work out an order of priorities (which may well not be related to their relative intrinsic importances), and the appropriate order of learning may vary from child to child. Which leads to the fourth point —one whose obviousness seems to make it all the easier to ignore: children reach readiness at different times. Fifthly, any concern with readiness is incomplete without a consideration of the possible formation of bad habits that have subsequently to be unlearned. We shall return to those points after discussing *preparatory* teaching.

Earlier, we reached the conclusion that the stronger a child's sense of an audience for whom he is writing, the more ready he will be to receive instruction in the conventions of presentation. Helping to create this sense of an audience in a child is, therefore, a prior task to teaching him what the reader's particular needs are. In this light, the frequency with which a teacher reads a child's work with the child beside him, or has it read to him by the child, and the frequency with which a child's writing is read out to other children or is pinned up on the wall, take on an added significance. Not only are these procedures generally encouraging, they also constitute specific preparation. And they will be further complemented if the teacher occasionally writes when his children write, and then reads out or lets them read out what he has written.* For the sense of an audience involves a sense of reciprocity: it will be reinforced if teacher and children occasionally exchange roles in this way. On the other hand, if a teacher merely collects up a class's writing at the end of a lesson, and hands it back the next day or the day after that, this will tend to arrest any developing sense of an audience. And with children whose sense of an audience is minimal, it is particularly crass to not only do this but also cover their work with corrections; for this must tend to condition them into *not wanting* an audience. It is safe to say that, especially in the early terms of the junior school but also afterwards, it is generally better for a child to receive a very brief face-to-face response to what he has written as soon as possible after he has written it (and that this response be usually an encouraging one) than for the teacher, even with the seemingly enlightened

---

* What we are advocating has nothing to do with the provision by the teacher of models. Nevertheless, we realize that the practice could amount to this in effect, and that therefore it could be dangerous—especially if the teacher's writing approaches the 'formal' or 'poetic' in Professor Britton's sense; or if he saw good writing as, for example, a matter of vividness gained by inserting 'good' adjectives.

intention of wanting to sort out what corrections the child is ready for, to postpone the encounter for a few hours—or days, as sometimes happens. We are not seeking to abrogate the teacher's traditional function of correcting mistakes; rather, we want to emphasize the need to prepare for such correction, by increasing children's receptivity. The means which we have mentioned so far are indirect, but they can become gradually more direct to some purpose. Here it is convenient to refer to Margaret Spencer's article where she says, on page 138, of one piece of writing:

> The total immersion of the teller results in a version which has great sweep and power. It drives on, if somewhat confusedly for the over-sophisticated reader.

She invites a comparison with an 'older child's attempts to retell a story about Romulus so that the characters and actions are clearly differentiated for the reader', and then comments:

> As the child's egocentrism declines, so he begins to put the reader in full possession of the facts of the tale, and the narrative flood decreases.

This suggests to us that early direct approaches with a child to the needs of a reader are best made chiefly in terms of *information* that he has omitted, rather than of ways, for example, that punctuation helps the reader along. If the teacher questions a child tactfully, almost by the way, about any informational gaps, the child will see this as a function of the teacher's interest, not as an indication that he has Done Something Wrong; and the practice will almost certainly have a useful cumulative effect.

Our stress, then, is on a developmental approach. For only in this way can a teacher coherently take account both of the need to promote the self-discovery that writing can be, and of the fact that skilled writing finally involves successful communication. But having said this, we do not want the reader to infer that we are advocating a rigidly linear developmental approach. For instance, we can see no harm and some point in a teacher telling a child, soon after he has started to write a few words at a time connectedly, that it is usual to start a piece of writing with a capital letter and to end it with a full stop. Similarly, he might tell the child that the names of people begin with a capital letter, and, a little later, say the same about towns or countries. A little later still, once the child was able to form all lower case letters satisfactorily, the teacher could go on to explain that capital letters don't come in the middle of words (that is, unless the child's name were McIntyre ...). But it would be quite inappropriate to attempt to teach a child at the same stage that all sentences begin with a capital letter and end with a full-stop; or that all proper nouns begin with a capital letter. The first would involve the teacher in an explanation of what constitutes a sentence; the second, in a definition of the difference between proper nouns and other nouns. These far from simple matters would almost certainly be far beyond the child's understanding; and any partial understanding that the child did achieve would, at this stage, amount to clutter.

With regard to learning 'readiness', we agree with recent thinking which holds that, generally speaking, it can be a dangerous concept. By the time a child *shows* that he is ready to learn something, he may be more than ready. However, we see teaching the conventions as a special case. There is a sharp distinction to be made between teaching *them* and teaching, for example, the operation of mathematical concepts. In addition to the relative unimportance of the conventions, we would point to the fact that, if children write engagedly about what concerns them, there will be no redundancy of the kind that occurs when children go on practising a mathematical operation after it has become a firm part of their knowledge. In other words, if children go on writing about things that concern them in ignorance of a certain convention, even after they have reached the stage when teaching of that convention would be meaningful to them, this will not (given a qualification we mention below) do any harm:

the basic activity will be taking place. We believe that, if in doubt about a child's readiness to be taught a convention, a teacher should postpone teaching it—or, at least, that the teacher should be very ready to give up immediately he senses a child failing to grasp what he is attempting to teach. To continue would be likely to induce an anxiety in the child which would issue in a false sense of priorities when writing, and would probably be counter-productive in its own cause, too.

We know how easy it is to act as though a child's incompetence at the age of eight will stay with him for life unless something is done more or less immediately about it—especially when that is the dominant attitude of his parents, and Open Day is in the offing. But we want to emphasize that there is no pedagogical justification for the primary school teacher to be in a hurry over the conventions. We believe that many children go on committing an array of habitual errors—such as forming plurals by adding an apostrophe s, or putting inverted commas round indirect speech—until they leave school, precisely because their primary school teachers felt they just had to teach them these things—otherwise they wouldn't know them when they left school . . . Of course, a child can pick up bad habits unnecessarily *by default* of the teacher; but here again a distinction has to be made—in particular, between spelling and punctuation.

In order to write, whether just for himself or to communicate to somebody else, a child has to attempt the spelling of every word he uses: he is bound to spell or misspell each word, he cannot not-spell it. On the other hand, as the Clare passage showed, it is quite possible to not-punctuate. The acquisition of competence in spelling will, therefore, characteristically involve a much greater element of *un*learning—unlearning of habitual misusages—than the acquisition of competence in punctuation. 'But what,' a teacher might ask, 'does this mean in practice?' This question cannot be answered satisfactorily by us: a teacher simply has to learn to judge how much concern for the conventions he can evince without it beginning to get in the way, without it inducing in a child a false sense of priorities, or confusion. This will vary, perhaps considerably, from child to child—according to his age, his ability, his interest, his flexibility, his aspirations; the effects of his past experience, of his parents' expectations, of his friends' attitudes; his attitudes to reading, to writing, to learning generally, to the teacher, to the school.... The list could be much extended. Here is an obvious area for joint, comparative study by all the teachers in a school (or perhaps two groups of them, if the school has more than, say, eight classes). Time spent for an hour each week on such matters would be incomparably more interesting, and incomparably more useful from every point of view, than the same time spent by each teacher in isolation on what is commonly regarded as the drudgery of marking.

Reference to the ways in which children vary leads us to stress that the teaching of the conventions should largely consist of discussion with individual children or—less often—with pairs or groups. 'Readiness' is an individual matter; and the occasion when it is especially appropriate to discuss a given point must also, usually, be an individual matter. Moreover, we have no doubt that strident markings on a child's work, in addition to being offensive as defacement, often have as their chief effect the reassurance of the teacher that he is not failing to do his job (cf. 'Take out your reading books'); and that if corrections are not actually discussed with a child, they are likely to have *no* effect other than the latter and the alienation of the child.* It must be very dispiriting to come to expect more or less the same old number of red marks to the page, the same old brief comment (give or take a 'quite' or a 'very') and list of 'corrections' at the bottom: it must surely be remarkable if the child's response *isn't* mechanical. Of course, a teacher cannot properly discuss a child's work with him anything like as frequently as he would wish, but this

---

* See M. L. Peters, *Spelling: Taught or Caught?*, (Routledge and Kegan Paul) on the need to draw children's attention specifically to their errors. This book contains much useful information and advice on the teaching of spelling. Although it is not altogether free of the attitude, 'the earlier the better', on balance its priorities are similar to ours.

167

is not a reason for allowing his staple response to that work to be little or no more than a dull registering of trivial errors after the event. Let the extent (in terms of time spent) of the teacher's response, the extent of his engagement with a child and his writing, vary considerably. If necessary, let the majority of his responses amount to no more than quickly reading through a given piece of writing with the author beside him soon after he has written it, offering a brief comment (as encouraging as possible) which takes up something the child has written so as to show him that he has engaged with his reader, and initialling the piece—commonly without mentioning any errors. This will at least leave the teacher time for a full discussion with *each* child *sometimes*. And if writing is not a 'special' activity, accordingly time-tabled, but something that is going on most of the time somewhere in the classroom, then 'sometimes' may well be several times a week.

We are not meaning to imply that when a teacher takes an opportunity to respond fully to a piece of writing, this necessarily involves him in questioning the child directly and closely about its substance. Sometimes, when the child has committed a confidence to paper or when the main burden of a piece is not its surface meaning,* tact will demand that the teacher approaches the substance indirectly, or moves away from it tangentially, associatively.

There can be a point in a child, most commonly after he has spent several terms in the junior school, writing out corrected spellings in a personal spelling book; but this should generally be restricted to occasions when the teacher is able to discuss more important matters as well. Otherwise, the child will be justified in feeling that the only or main consequence of his effort—and hence, the purpose of his effort—is a further task, one that is mechanical and boring. The teacher should select carefully from among the child's errors when he has made more than one or two, and should then regard his selec-

---

* On this subject, see, for instance, Ruth Griffiths, *Imagination in Early Childhood*, (Routledge and Kegan Paul).

tions as one, relatively unimportant element in the matter to be discussed. What is fundamental is involvement by the teacher in the *substance* of the child's writing. Such involvement guarantees to the child that corrections are worth taking seriously: it will tend to maintain or renew his interest, often to the point where he *wants* to produce a fair copy. With older juniors, this is the moment when some teaching in punctuation is likely to be most effective. With younger children, and less able older children, it will usually be more appropriate to discuss mainly or exclusively other aspects of presentation (in particular, how the fair copy might be decorated or illustrated), with a view to fostering the sense of an audience that we referred to earlier. We should perhaps emphasize that we are not advocating this sort of approach as a *strategy* for getting a child to learn the conventions, but as a *justification* for considering them at all.

In the last paragraph, we mentioned the decoration of fair copies; and, of course, there is no reason why first drafts should not be decorated and illustrated as well (as we have already said, the majority of them will be only drafts). Indeed, the practice is to be welcomed. Because writing is made up of non-iconic symbols (i.e. it is not picture-writing), it can be a relief or sustaining to a child to deal, part of the time, in the direct representation or embroidery of things he is writing or has written about.* The less experienced he is as a writer, the more likely this is to be so; but it remains true of many children long after they have become minimally proficient writers; and it would probably remain so much longer still if most children were not conditioned into believing that they 'can't draw' by the time they arrive at the secondary school or soon afterwards. (Everyone can draw. The notion that being able to draw means being able to produce life-like, 'realistic', representations of an object is an unfortunate, culturally determined prejudice.) Which brings us to the problem of hand-writing.

----

*This is not contradicted by the fact that it *can* be inept of a teacher to say unthinkingly: 'That's nice, dear; now do a drawing of it.' Sometimes all the creative effort a child can give to a subject for the time being may have been expended in the writing.

We feel that the less emphasis hand-writing—in small, using a pencil—receives in the infant school, the better. This is not because we regard hand-writing as unimportant: from the point of view of successful communication, there is a case for saying it is more important than spelling and punctuation.* It seems clear to us that the business of trying to manipulate a pencil satisfactorily can be a considerable hindrance to a child's initial engagement with written code; and, in addition, it seems a reasonable hypothesis that a year or two after a child has started school, when his co-ordination has much improved, is a better time for intensive teaching of hand-writing. We cannot deal here with techniques for teaching the formation of letters; nor, in fact, are we competent to deal properly with the larger practical questions that our view raises. All we can say here is that, in particular, the infant teacher and the teacher of backward juniors should enable his children to use as many ways to record written code as possible, in order to remove some of the pressure that ordinary hand-writing can produce. Materials produced by the Initial Literacy Project are very useful in this respect. In addition, transcription (not necessarily by the teacher) of taped dictation by a child, chalk on blackboards (or slates for that matter), and especially—if at all possible—typewriters† should be regarded as means of composing for daily use. A variety of this sort—and our list isn't meant to be exhaustive— will be enlivening, as well as a relief from pencil-pushing.

Throughout this article , we have discussed the teaching of the conventions in relation to the main business of composition. It might be inferred that all such teaching should be tied to what a child has written. Generally speaking this is so; but we want to make it clear that we are not necessarily against exercises, etc. In some measure,

---

* Thus, it matters much less if a teacher is unable to remember unerringly that e comes before i after c, than if his hand-writing is difficult to read.

† For a very relevant description of research, by Dr. O. K. Moore of Yale University, into the beneficial effects of using typewriters, instead of pencil or pen, for the early teaching of reading and writing, see John Downing (ed.), *The First International Reading Symposium*, pp. 12-15, (Cassell).

our attitude depends on the extent to which the understanding of a convention can be seen as a function, or an extension, of choosing 'what to say and how to say it' in Mr. Schiller's sense. Thus, we believe that punctuation will, essentially, be best learnt gradually from discussion with the teacher about particular pieces that a child has written. But occasional exercises can help even with punctuation. We are not thinking of the conventional sort, in which children are asked to insert capital letters, commas, inverted commas, question marks, full-stops, etc., in the right order, into inert sentences that a textbook writer or eleven-plus examiner has thought up specially. Many older juniors *can* be drilled into completing these efficiently. But it is our experience that there is often very little, if any, transfer of such expertize to their own writing. (To occasionally type out a piece by a child just as he has written it, and then to ask him to correct it in collaboration with a friend, is a different matter.) On the other hand, if a group of children were asked to punctuate a number of sentences similar to the one about a horse bolting on page 160, they should certainly gain something from the discussion that ensued when it was discovered that there was no right answer. Two or three exercises of this kind in the course of a term could help them to a proper respect for punctuation, *confirm* knowledge that they had already partially got, and hence perhaps influence them to use punctuation marks less haphazardly (for most children, the best time to do such exercises is in the last year or so of the junior school).

We are sure it is undesirable for there to be a continuous traffic of children coming up to the teacher for spellings while they write. It can happen that a child comes and asks for every other word: this cannot but get in the way of what he is about. Once or twice perhaps—but no more, unless the piece is especially long or technical. And in classes where all the children write at the same time, even moderate toing and froing can generate a usurping momentum. (Of course, we are not suggesting that a teacher should tell a child to sit down immediately if he has already been to him twice. What we have in mind is a largely tacit attitude prevailing in the class, which keeps *spelling* in its place.) Similarly, although we approve in principle of the use of dictionaries, we think they should be regarded, primarily, as a reading tool, rather than a writing tool.

In order to enable a child to use a dictionary effectively, it can be helpful for him to do a series of exercises on alphabetical order when he is ready (and all the children in a class, whether unstreamed or streamed, certainly will not be ready at the same time). Dictionary exercises in which a child finds out and writes down the 'meaning' of words that a dictionary gives are more questionable, for two reasons. First, they treat meanings in a void. Secondly, so-called 'junior' dictionaries are inevitably very arbitrary in their selection not only of words but of meanings. Which is why we said 'in principle' just now. A 'junior' dictionary can be as much a hindrance as a help to a child (more so than to an adult, who understands and can make allowances for the arbitrariness). Most if not all fourth year classrooms, and every junior school library, should have a set of the two-volume *Shorter Oxford Dictionary*, which briefly gives the life histories of words and meanings. Once a child is not daunted by the sight of large pages packed with words, it can actually be easier to use, as well as be incomparably more exciting. (One of us once found himself discussing original passages from Chaucer and *Sir Gawayne and the Grene Knight*—and comparing them with the Penguin translations—with a group of ten-year-olds in response to interest that ensued when the *Shorter Oxford Dictionary* was introduced into the classroom.)

Basically, our attitude is that the conventions, and spelling in particular, should not become tin-cans that a child drags around with him whenever he is concerned with writing. Because of this, and because of the arbitrariness of written code, it seems to us desirable that the learning of spelling should be separated to some extent from composition. We see no harm and likely gain in a teacher looking with each child, intensively and systematically for a few minutes twice a week, at words and families of words that the child has had difficulty with;

and sometimes this will be best done with a pair or group of children. We see no harm and likely gain in a child learning by rote spellings from a personal spelling book, and then testing himself with the help of a friend, for five minutes each day. There is a place, too, for occasional word games that have the aim of establishing spelling regularities and irregularities. The important thing is that the procedures adopted should become neither a burden nor a distraction. In other words, let the traditional priorities be turned on their head.

In recent years, there has been much talk of 'creative writing'; but there has been very little discussion, let alone systematic study, of what constitutes progress in *engaged* writing. Because teachers have no clear notions of how skilled writing behaviour in an eleven-year-old might differ from skilled writing behaviour in a seven-year-old, it is not surprising that they should fall back on surface competences for their criterion of progress, or—to put it another way—that 'parental pressures' (real or imagined) for the maintenance of 'standards', defined in terms of such competences, should exert an undue influence. Nor is it surprising that 'creative writing' should often be separated off from other classroom activities, and in consequence stagnate or take gimmicky directions.

Professor Britton's essay provides one way into the matter; and 'What are they up to?' offers the beginnings of a systematic, comprehensive account. We need many more such studies. But what is equally necessary is that teachers should meet regularly to compare each other's experiences and to thrash out appropriate expectations. It is absurd to suggest that if, for example, playtime continued from the mid-afternoon break till going home time once a fortnight, in order to allow extra time for this, that the children's education would suffer.

If discussion of children's writing, and other aspects of their work, took place regularly, it seems certain that problems of organization would soon become a preoccupation. For we have no doubt at all that the approaches we have outlined in this article, and which are indicated throughout this book, can be followed much more readily and fully in a classroom where there is no time-table of the traditional kind, and where the class is very seldom working as one unit. We appreciate that to operate in this way puts a heavy burden on the teacher, and demands from him considerable efficiency in the organization of his time. But we also believe that it is a condition of really efficient teaching. The knowledge and the morale to pursue this teaching will come only when teachers collaborate with each other as comprehensively as possible.

Isolated teachers giving class English lessons, and doing their marking in the dinner hour, just will not do.

The articles 'What Are They Up To?' and 'Spelling Etc.' demonstrate that when we use language we are subject to three often conflicting pressures (and this conflict is never more acute than in the learning/teaching situation, the pupil/teacher relationship). First, we may be representing some part of our experience to *ourselves*, perhaps hoping to make some sense of it. Suzanne Langer has pointed out that symbolizing—representing our inner vision in movement, visual art, language—is a fundamental urge, almost an instinct, and much of our language behaviour expresses this need. Secondly, we may use language to communicate with other people. In serving both these purposes—to represent to ourselves and to communicate—our language, at its best, will be rooted in our individual personalities and backgrounds. But there is a third pressure working on us: we may feel pressure to satisfy an impersonal demand of 'society' (which will mean a class or sector *within* society) or of a subject 'discipline'. Many parents and teachers (and so, in turn, many children) are highly susceptible to this third, potent sort of pressure: it can easily become the source of a parent's or teacher's explicit criteria of language usage, and lead to coercion of children towards stereotype forms —coercion that is often inappropriate, and harmful. (For further discussion of writing as an activity and the teacher's response to children's work, see the articles by Leslie Stratta and Anthony Jones in *Writing*—Vol. 3, No. 3, Autumn 1969, of N.A.T.E.'s journal *English in Education*, (O.U.P. and N.A.T.E.).

The publication of *Letter to a Teacher* by the School of Barbiana (Penguin) is timely for our purpose of drawing together the last threads of this book, and salutary. For one thing, it calls in question the assumptions of many of us who advocate (indeed, swear by) the need for aesthetic education in the forms of, for example, literature and drama.

Little Pierino, the doctor's son, has plenty of time to read fables. Not Gianni. He dropped out of your hands at fifteen. He is in a factory. He does not need to know whether it was Jupiter who gave birth to Minerva or vice versa.

His Italian literature course would have done better to include the contract of the metalworkers' union. Did you ever read it, Miss? Aren't you ashamed? It means the life of half a million families.

You keep telling yourselves how well educated you are. But you have all read the same books. Nobody ever asks you anything different. (Page 31)

Probably this attack is aimed not so much at stories and poems themselves, as at the abuse of literature as a device that divides children from one another—at the *appropriation* of literature by the middle and upper classes. This appropriation is made through the trivial currency of 'what one ought to know *about*' literature, and by defining literature in terms of the hermetic category of 'The Arts', to gain access to which it is necessary to have Culture.* Nevertheless, the quotation does indicate the need to explain and justify with reference to *language development* (as this book has tried to do) the use of stories and poems and drama with children in school—the great majority of whom are not disposed to read meritorious books unprompted by their teachers.

Letter to a Teacher focusses attention on the way schools fail a high proportion of children by creating a gulf between themselves and those children who are most in need of the learning they have—or should have— to offer. In a system that is founded on testing and rejection, language is a critical and potentially crippling instrument. Too often the working class pupil becomes a victim of alien middle class language behaviour: †

---

* Cf. the comments by D. W. Harding quoted on page 151.

† For the relevant references to the socio-linguistic work of Basil Bernstein, see page 53. In particular, the article, 'A Critique of the Concept of "Compensatory Education"', tackles controversially the

Besides, we should settle what correct language is. Languages are created by the poor, who then go on renewing them forever. The rich crystallize them in order to put on the spot anybody who speaks in a different way. Or in order to make him fail exams.

You say that little Pierino, daddy's boy, can write well. But of course; he speaks as you do. He is part of the firm. (Pages 23/4.)

Some teachers may feel that this analysis does not account for the working class children who write well and the middle class children who don't; but the experiences that Connie Rosen describes in the next article certainly support the view that the young teacher with his record of academic success has a radical adjustment to make— in his expectations of other people's language and his attitudes towards it, and in his own use of language. The adjustment is partly a matter of understanding what it is to be a child; but also, what it is to be a child whose social environment, and therefore language environment, is very *different* from anything he has directly experienced before.

---

question of how much a teacher should respect the language that a child brings to school. See also *The Language of Failure* (*English in Education*, Vol. 4, No. 3, Autumn, 1970, O.U.P. and N.A.T.E.).

CLASSROOM ENCOUNTER

Connie Rosen

> D cabbage as pattern e wa k wolea s pattern il the ke
> I etin in school at Vola Iamoha af I a mon a I go tia of tia
> I c insa IM it Ig d tia Di tit ic d otic a the I come c the
> theorad coa the Igine ra come klo at neigh ih the fr so
> the tv

This was written by Edgerton, a seven-year-old boy, for David, one of the students on the three-year course. I would not like to suggest that this is the usual standard of literacy that the students meet, but it would be true to say that in every school within a ten mile radius of our College, students are likely to meet some children with this degree of difficulty in school learning. The children often come from overcrowded home conditions, the majority of the parents work in semi-skilled or unskilled jobs, the Jamaican children often suffer from the anxieties and isolation caused by racial discrimination, and the schools are very old. It's very curious, the effect of buildings on one's thinking. There are interesting displays of fabrics and pots and plants and books when there's glass and timber and the school's on an intimate, domestic scale. When there are great lengths of cement corridors, children and staff seem to fly to the classrooms and leave the cemented places empty and unadorned. And when there are three floors of brick and tile and spiralling stairs as is the case in many city schools, then no matter how clean or how warm or how solid, the school still has an institutional feel, and somehow still conveys the Board school idea of teaching reading, writing and arithmetic to the poor. So there it is: the children who live in the worst conditions in the centres of industrial cities usually have the worst school conditions, the greatest turnover of staff, and very often suffer from the most limited conception of Primary education. When there's stream and woodland and farm, it's likely that the teachers will use the environment in their teaching, but in so many old city schools, little is done to bring children closer to a natural environment, let alone their own. One finds schools a stone's throw from the River Thames where it's thought a waste of time when the students take the children out to look at the river, an old church or a historic building. In this area, one feels that the children's lives are filled with noise, dissension and crowded places, and so very, very often school is filled with remedial reading, spelling, English exercises and sums. In some areas children are suffering from certain deprivations in the home background and the school compensates for these, but in other areas the same kind of children with the same kinds of deprivation have the additional handicap of a deprived education. The answer does not rest with i.t.a., closed circuit television or teaching French to five-year-olds. There aren't any short cuts and there aren't any easy answers. Part of the answer lies in understanding that children who find school work difficult need more time, part of the answer lies in really understanding that children who have difficulty in reading and writing need to talk more with adults. They need to share a variety of interesting experiences with adults, and we need to look at the quality of relationship between adults and children. The adults talked about in this article were students on a three-year course and post-graduate students* doing a one-year course in Primary education, and some understanding of *their* difficulties is also necessary.

I suppose quite simply what one hopes to achieve in the language work must begin with the children. This is even more true when considering children like Edgerton. It is scarcely surprising that students at College who have had so little contact with young children should find it so difficult to adjust to the scale of their world. Fortunately we have all experienced childhood ourselves and it helps if the students begin there.... 'A white swan with black eyes and a yellow beak which rocked backwards and forward and which I had tried to paint green on one side'.... 'Next door to my friend's house there was a hardware shop. It always smelt of chopped wood,

* In this article I am much indebted to the work of my students at the University of London Goldsmith's College during the years 1967-69.

and the small bundles were stacked against the counter —I used to like pulling small splinters from the short sticks which were wound round with wire. It seemed to me, in fact, that all the shop was made of wood—wooden floorboards, dark polished wood counter with chips out of it. Even the owner reminded me of wood. His name was Mr. Yule and he always wore a tan coloured overall —I remember thinking he reminded me of a large stick of wood himself, stuck in his cramped little shop.'

These are taken from autobiographical pieces written by the students at the beginning of their course. It serves many purposes: it is a reminder of the preoccupations of children, and at the same time, helps towards an understanding of the task of writing. We discuss the question of who they are writing for. What purpose it serves. What sort of comments they anticipate—comments on style, paragraphing, etc., or content. And, perhaps, most important of all is their surprise at the kinds of recollection that seem to come to the surface and the discoveries they make about themselves. They find that the preparatory talk helps, and that the reading and sharing of each other's reminiscences stimulates so much they thought they'd forgotten. But this talking and writing about themselves is only a very small beginning.

Consider the problems of these young people. They belong to the minority group who have been highly successful in their own schooling (successful in terms of passing all the exams needed to take them to the next set of exams) and they meet children like Edgerton whose piece is quoted at the beginning of this article.

We must of necessity have some investment, and even some degree of pride, in the kind of influences that have made us what we are. It would be unnatural if students, who for ten years have jumped the hoops of an eleven-plus examination, O Levels, A Levels and then a degree course, should not feel that this had all been very beneficial, especially if they have enjoyed it sufficiently to return to teaching. Life becomes even more complicated if their memories of their own Primary schools have been full of coming top in spelling tests, long division, team marks, cups for football and netball and slaving obediently covering acres of exercise books getting it right. Apart from anxieties due to some parental pressures, they are scarcely likely to have met the kind of difficulties and failures that many children experience in the schools in which they do their teaching practice, and only a small minority of students can possibly have any notion at all of the home conditions of the children. And, unfortunately, none of us knows the feeling of being the wrong colour. It is always surprising in the circumstances—and a constant credit to the imagination and sensitivity of young people—how many of them leap the barriers and achieve, even on the shortest acquaintance with young children, a real warmth and an understanding relationship with them. Of those that do achieve this, some probably do so because they are interested in children, in what they say and do; some because they feel protective, and because they can share the children's interest in the world around them.

The students work with a small group of children one morning a week for a term. The following extracts are taken from their comments on the children. The school is very overcrowded. The headmaster and staff are very helpful and friendly to anyone who comes to the school —to each other, children, students, visitors. Forty per cent of the school population are immigrants, and many of the children come from extremely difficult backgrounds, divided homes, overcrowded homes, homes that are harmonious neither internally nor socially.

Deirdre writes:

> Stephen is a coloured boy of seven and appears very shy and subdued. This may be due to the fact that he is coloured and he feels inferior. However, he does not work to his capacity and when asked to do a set piece of work, he prefers to do something else and then join the others. His antics round the classroom and general behaviour could all be for attention, but his motives are generally quite a mystery. He reads well but is just lazy and noisy. His maths work is remedial but if put under strict supervision, he could benefit greatly from group work.

181

Whilst in the group, Stephen often wanders off due to not being able to concentrate on a particular topic for any length of time. He tends to be mischievous but it may be to draw attention to himself.

When we played Snakes and Ladders he managed to count well but was accused of cheating by the other children when he claimed to have won. His art work, which he seemed to enjoy more than anything else was most pleasing and here, he never wanted to do other things. He worked quietly but in English, his logic was strange:

I play with gun I brot a gun today I brot it and it fies potatoes and caps and water we let of the caps and made a big bang.

Towards the end of the term Deirdre wrote:

In Art, they all recognized the fossil I had brought in and Brian said that it had been an animal, millions of years ago, when there were dinosaurs. It had been left in the ground and eventually turned to stone. The paintings were very realistic with good colour. At the end, however, Jonathon proceeded to go round the whole class showing the fossil to literally everyone telling them all about it. Apparently they had heard about fossils quite recently on the radio. Stephen's picture was exceptionally good and he appears to be the type of pupil who gets on better with things without asking anyone anything. His work is slow but with due praise and encouragement, he could do as well as the other children.

David D. wrote:

By way of a further change I decided to do some art work with them by studying a cabbage. This turned out to be a good sevenpenny-halfpenny investment. I cut it up into pieces so that each child had a piece. I asked them to observe what they saw and then draw the patterns in magnified form on their sheet of paper. Surprisingly Edgerton, who does not show a great deal of intelligence in academic work was the most successful in creating a pattern of some complexity that showed many signs of close observation. On the other Dennis who is usually quite bright was obviously not working at his best. I asked them to write about the cabbage that was in front of them—how it felt, looked, smelt, etc. I was pleasantly surprised at their work. Just when things started to go flat, Nicholas discovered an insect that had obviously been on one of the leaves and immediately there was renewed interest and a number of questions were asked.

Edgerton—A very quiet and shy boy who showed much reticence in oral work. I was never able to get to know him as much as the others partly because of his reticence, but mainly because he was absent for four weeks out of the seven. I was unable to discover whether his silence was due to his shyness or because he was unable to communicate. His English was not very clear and when he spoke I often had to ask him to repeat what he was saying or wait till one of the others translated.

His work was not too good, but at least he always tried very hard. However, when he did me a drawing of a piece of cabbage I was amazed at the detail and fluency with which he was able to draw. I stopped the work to let everybody look at his attempt and this gave him a good deal of pleasure. He was anxious to take it to show the class teacher and she gave him extra praise and encouragement which acted as a further incentive.

On the whole I got the impression that he was not a happy child. He always looked lost and forlorn and seemed to be treated by the others as something of an outsider. He was unfortunate because he could not communicate either by speaking or by writing. He never wrote sense—his sentences were just a string of odd letters and squiggles. One of the others summed up his situation when she said, 'Oh, don't take any notice of him, he always writes rubbish like that.'

D cabbage as pattern e wa k wolea s pattern il the ke I–etin in school at Vola Iamoha af I a mon a I go tia of tia I c insa IM it Ig d tia Di tit ic d otic a the I come c the theorad coa the Igine ra come klo at neigh ih the fr so the tv

Joe began with her group of six children looking at autumn leaves, and Olric wrote:

In the Autumn the leaves fall off the trees the leaves are crunchy the leaves are green and the leaves and yellow

and Tangey Mehmet Fehmi wrote:

In Autumn the leaves fall off the trees
              and brown red yellow
They felt soft
They felt soft
One day. There was a little glie and sth went in to The garden. and sthe pegdedt the leaves off the ground

and it is a credit to the kind of relationship Joe was able to create, and the way the children accepted the student, that Stephen wrote:

we looked at some chrysanthemums smelt like ming and orange poureb into pepper They were soft but hard in the middle They Felt Fluffy They were white pink and yellow

Back in college one of the students became very agitated. He'd read a poem to his group of children and asked them to write a poem. He then read with some distaste a piece of work from a child which he considered utterly confused, utter nonsense and quite lacking in standard. He seemed very keen on standards.

> a dog pit sume gun palda in is ier and his bran broc
> and is hed blo of the smoc went up a be come a
> long and the smoc mad the be fho daln ded
> (A dog put some gun powder in his ear and his
> brain broke and his head blew off the smoke
> went up a bee came along and the smoke made
> the bee fall down dead)

The rest of the group dealt with him, explained that he was over-critical, he hadn't helped the children sufficiently, he was expecting too much, that he himself couldn't write a poem at the drop of a hat—and Joe read the piece about the chrysanthemums and said she couldn't have thought of anything like that herself.

David B. had a group of six children too, of whom one, Paul, was somewhat difficult:

> They've done number patterns and made a dice
> and did some crayon and wash pictures. They
> drew leaves and made a block graph of the different
> colours and Paul contributed nothing. They made
> some symmetrical patterns with paint and at last
> Paul writes:
>> the pattn look like Frnunkstien
>> Junior and Buzz and Frnauknstien
>> does all the work for Junior
>> and that in inPosballs
>> and tht in inPosballs Help
>> Junior and Buzz and Junior and Buzz
>> Help I the Inposball and F is end
>>> of PaRt one

And it's really difficult to know what has happened between the student and Paul except that the student has a philosophical persistence and pleasure in Paul's progress. The last piece written by Paul after a walk to the shops read as follows:

> we wnt for a walk to goe some shors and we
> have now to write about it. Sweets shop and

185

food shoP and A cake shoP and A bread-Shop
and Pet-Shop and saw some PuPPies and
PuPPies Playing With each other and I saw a
broken car and a engine in the car and alsatiand
and I was scared of the alsation doG

In these meetings with the small groups of children,
the students have taken them to look at the cement mixer,
the pet shop, and the park. They have taken in things
for the children to look at and talk about, have read
them poems and stories, have worked on number apparatus and drawn and painted. They have talked with them
about their families, their pets, their interests and have
mounted the children's work in books so that the children
can take pleasure in the final results. We spend some
tutorial time talking about the children and what they're
doing together. We have looked at suitable poems and
story books. We have examined readers. We have discussed the kind of help the children need to get their
thoughts on to paper. We look as though we're all travel-
ling along together very amicably with the idea that they
provide the experience, the talk, the materials and the
help. It's all very enjoyable and the children look forward
to their visits. But the students are cautious. This can't
be English, this cement mixer and chrysanthemums and
Autumn leaves, this talking and painting and drawing
and making. There is still a long, long road ahead.

I think the road I'm trying to travel, and I'm hoping
they're accompanying me, is one of understanding that
they're not teaching English but that they're helping
children with the whole business of living and that the
language work is part of the living. It has to do with
learning the smell of chrysanthemums by smelling them,
of learning that children talk to strange adults if they feel
at home with them, and that you just can't set to with a
preconceived programme of exercises for teaching the
mother tongue.

We have arrived at second school practice and many
of the students seem to be fired with enthusiasm about
the poetry. They read it to the children and are thrilled
with the poems the children write for them. On my tour

around I find myself suggesting that there have been other poets since Tennyson, Masefield and Flecker and that there are several stories besides the *Wind in the Willows, Alice in Wonderland* and the *Pied Piper of Hamelin* that might contain something more relevant to Primary school children in the nineteen seventies. There is no doubt, however, that something is astir. David talks about poems the children have written and put to music on chime bars. I ask him if he can record it, but he's feeling either too harassed or as unused to this electronic age as I am. Jane has been reading Greek myths and they've been acting out the Trojan horse—especially the bit where they have to creep into it very quietly, which was a great help.

Carol has been teaching a C stream group of nine- and ten-year-olds. She comments on some poems arising from the work on the five senses and quotes:

> Sandpaper, sandpaper, play me a tune
> Play it sweet, play it rough, play it neat,
> Clear as it is, rough as it feels.
>
> Lesley

> Fur is soft as rock is hard
> fur is warm as snow is cold
> fur is as nice as nice
> Pity pillows aren't made of fur
> Because it keeps you warm at night.

She tells them the story of Orpheus and Eurydice. It's significant that she discovered that telling them the story in this case was better than reading it. But then she asks them lots of questions like 'What is a lute?' 'Of course I got the reply that a lute is money. Their written replies to the questions were quite good.... At the end of the story Stephen asked me, "Why didn't Orpheus kill himself after Eurydice died and then he could have been with her?".'

She has doubts about the questions she has asked and

187

wonders whether they have been of any help. The question that Stephen asked seems to be much nearer to the heart of the matter. Perhaps it would be better if they thought up their own questions.

At the end of the practice Carol writes:

> I asked the children to choose one particular lesson they had had with me and write about it. I was interested in their reactions to my very different type of teaching from that to which they had become accustomed. I was a little surprised at the piece of writing I received from this work—most of the children chose either my drama lessons, Movement lessons or art and craft ones to write about. A few did comment on my maths lesson and a few on my poetry lessons, especially the sound poems. There were comments like, 'We like acting best because we all have parts.' 'I played the eagle in one lesson.' 'We like doing things like measuring the area of things in the classroom.' 'We like making model cubes.'
>
> Some said my lessons were easy and that's why they liked them and others said they liked it because 'We talk about what we are doing to Miss Brooks.'

They liked all the doing and making and acting and they liked talking things over with Miss Brooks. It doesn't seem to be a bad idea to do the things they feel happy and confident in.

Carol commented on one boy:

> Stephen was hardly ever at school, a delicate child from a difficult background who visited a child psychiatrist twice a week. He was in the remedial maths group and was the slowest reader in the class. But he was knowledgeable and took part in class discussions. His writing was practically non-existent but he wrote this poem for me in my first lesson on poetry:

A lif on the wind
It witherd
It dide and it was
bernt to ash.

There does however, among the students, seem to be a great preoccupation with 'good words', and 'good words' seem to be three syllable ones. I ask what makes a three syllable word better than a one or two syllable word. It seems to me that any word, short or long, has different shades of meaning in relation to the other words around it and to the circumstances in which it's being used, but the students don't seem to be very convinced about this. Perhaps the children will be able to make this point clear. Pamela, who had been talking to the children about the sea, wrote in her note-book: 'No one used the words I mentioned like lapping, choppy, tossing or words from the poems to any degree.' But I notice that one of the pieces she quotes is:

I felt some shells. Some of the shells are rough and some shells smooth. I felt some seaweed It felt like rubber Seaweed is a dark browny colour. Seaweed is not Dry But it is Wet and Slimy. I Felt some PeBBles Some PeBBles Are rough and some Are sMooth I listened to a shell and it sounded to me as if it was windy and that the tide was going out.

Perhaps what happens is that when the student grows qualified, old and determined, the children will write that the choppy waves were tossing and lapping round their feet, and they lose faith in the shell that 'sounded to me as if it was windy and that the tide was going out'.

Marilyn too decides that she intends to widen the children's vocabulary. She gives the children the following exercises and sets them out with a decided aim, 'To widen the vocabulary, particularly of descriptive terms which are more vivid and vital than the usual verbs based on "to go", etc.' The children are to substitute some words for other words in the following sentences:

189

The fireworks *went up* into the air
The gunpowder *went off* with a bang
He *looked closely* at the old manuscript
The waterfall *fell into* the lake
The fish *swam quickly under the* riverbank

It is sad that she thought of doing it at all, but it's understandable. There are enough text books on the market explaining that this is what has to be done, and many, many teachers who think it does good. I am puzzled. If you haven't any alternative ways of saying these things, how do you do the exercise, and what's so bad about 'looking closely' at the old manuscript? I wonder how often those ten-year-old children from a Plowden Priority school in Camberwell have looked at old manuscripts. But there is progress. Marilyn discovered something for herself:

> This lesson was taken with the whole of the class and for many it was too advanced and they could not comprehend what was really needed. For those who did understand, it did reveal what very limited vocabulary the children have and the frugality of the teaching in sentence structure and punctuation.

However, she's a determined lass and continues on the sentence structure and punctuation. She tells them 'to make up suitable sentences using these words to the best of their ability . . . scurried, panted, ancient, darkening, vivid, billowing, verdant, tempestuous, caressed, threatening, lapped, fluttered'. But there's still time and the next entry is really in quite a different spirit, and in spite of the attachment to descriptive words, there is progress:

> Observation of objects under magnifying glasses.
> Each child to contribute one word descriptive of their object to put on the board as a basic vocabulary.
> To encourage a freedom of expression and writing that all children can achieve.

This lesson went particularly well, [...]
who normally are less able in Englis[...]
did their best here. Their vocabulary [...]
while coupled with close observation [...]
To many of the children this was a n[...]
for writing. The results were most [...]
especially when considering these wer[...]
There is great potential in this field.

She has been extremely hard working and conscientious and has made comments on each of the children:

Bevan. No in family 5. Position 5th. Hobbies
 Cricket and Football
Interest in School—Craft
Attitude to peers—has many friends.
Father's occupation—He does not know his father
Mother's occupation—Mother works at a factory
and comes home late, so sisters cook and feed the
family.
Helpful—tends to sulk and is an exhibitionist. Has
home background difficulties. His written work is
very poor and he cannot decline the verbs. His
very instability hinders any progress he could
make. Occasionally he appears very young and he
talks in a soft high-pitched little voice that he
knows is appealing.

Bevan writes this story for her:

There was a long hill. A on that hill there live
ten birds. Every day they had to fish for they
food. so the mother fly out of her nest to get
the food. and the father gard them. When the
mother came back and feed the babies. The father
bring food for him and there mother. A month
after the had to come out of there nest to fly.
all the babies came out except one. That one die
in the nest.

There's no doubt about it, communication is a very, very

ficult business. How to convince Marilyn that there couldn't possibly be any question of putting 'verdant' or 'darkening' into this piece? How to convince her of the feeling in the story of the mother bird and the baby birds who *did* have a father to bring food? How to convince her that the story is significant to the child and that the only response to it is sympathy and praise for the achievement?

Joe decided that 'A book of fascinating words will be compiled. This is a list of interesting words linked with topic work which are in their class dictionaries, which they can look up and find out the meaning of and which also can be used in their imaginative work.'

I discover that these fascinating words include words like 'iridescent' that can be used to describe the crystals they've been making and studying. Barbara says that a child in her class wrote that the 'night came creeping slowly like a worm' and someone else had written about the 'quiet moon'. But Joe describes Christopher and quotes a piece of writing he has done for her:

> Christopher—a restless over-active boy who will get up and wander out of the class doing tasks of his own making if not watched. He enters little into class activities and seems to be always thinking of other things. Fiddles and wastes time and cannot settle down to any task unless he has supervision. Seems to be outside the class activities and has few friends. Needs constant attention. Father—office worker. Mother—works.

> My dove pippi is a greyish white she is a small breek their are two of them they eat wild bird seed they love nuts in it best the two Doves like us they have to eggs they soon will hatch they Change evry day and they donnt vite we clean them out every day they fly in our house but they make a mess on the floor our cat does not like them she is scared of the doves the doves live in a cage for the winter in the summer we put them in the shed they fly freely in the shed

the doves starts to fly around but the doves do not keep flying they have to land.

Joe writes of Peter:

> Unhappy, withdrawn child, plays about a lot and is often spiteful to others. Doesn't get on well with father. Poor financially. Responds to affection. Badly scalded his face (during practice) on his hot water bottle. Did not complain but tried to avoid attention. Shy and withdrawn.
> Father invalid. Mother works full-time.

Peter has written:

> We done some tie dying on the 2nd February and Miss Aukett gave us some red ink but it did not work because we did not put any salt in it. But we have some blue dye and it was right. And I did not tie the wool very tite and mine did not come out when i put it in the red and i was very disappointed that mine did not went the first time. Then I put it in to the blue and tied the wool tie and it worked when i took it out and we had to rinse it out then i was satisfide.

Deirdre says she wishes she didn't have a Yorkshire accent and indeed one of the children had asked her if she was English. What with the preoccupation with 'good words' and increasing vocabulary and Deirdre's Yorkshire accent, I think it might be a good idea to have another voice. I ask Mr. R to come and talk to them and explain that he must deal with questions of accent, dialect, standard English, modern grammar—in fact to give a year's course of linguistics in one session. The students listen very intently but there seems to be a great deal that bothers them. What are you left to teach if you don't do lists of good words, parts of verbs, spelling, analysing poetry for metre and rhythm and comprehension?

I didn't expect Mr. R to work miracles in one session

but felt he would do more good by coming when the issues were hot than a standard lecture (or even course of lectures!) laid on irrespective of what was happening to the students. Certainly the reverberations of this session justified it. And a number of bogeys were laid, anxieties diminished and some of that weird folk-lore that passes for grammar and facts about language were at least undermined. It was a beginning.

It's not surprising that students should feel a sense of panic when confronted with children's backwardness in school work, particularly nowadays when so many people they meet in school and college are suggesting language exercises of one kind or another. The main problem is that attention is all too often directed to the reading and writing and not sufficiently to the talking. It may be that we cannot solve the problem without adequate nursery school provision. It may be that we cannot solve the problem without a much higher ratio of adults to children, especially those with difficulties. But many of the students quoted here have recorded a great deal of success with these children and this is only half a dozen meetings with them. Compare the piece of writing done by Paul for David B. at the end of the term with the first, the contrast between the children's response to Marilyn's exercises and the pieces they wrote for her later. Compare Dierdre's first comments on Stephen that he 'is just lazy and noisy' to her final comment after responding to his drawing that 'his work is slow but with due praise and encouragement, he could do as well as the other children.' And the pleasant surprise with which David D. received Edgerton's drawing of the cabbage did more for that boy than two terms of remedial reading. Well may they have been delighted with the children's poems, and the shared achievement of the piece of writing on the chrysanthemums, the story of the mother bird and the story of tie dyeing.

Perhaps some attention to language is necessary in stimulating an interest and curiosity in origins, sounds, changes in words, the way different people talk. It may be, with a better understanding of the way language works, students will be able to respond at the right time and in the right way to children's own comments and questions about language. It may be that we shall be able to think of language work as something more than accuracy in spelling and exercises divorced from children's own usage. We haven't really had a great deal of time to think about that yet. We've been busy trying to give the spoken language the greatest emphasis. We have been trying to look at the children, not as reading and writing problems but as human beings who must learn in their own way and in their own time. We have tried to avoid situations of failure and to create opportunities for success. The route sometimes seems extremely roundabout. It might begin with tie-dyeing, a visit to the pet shop, being a soldier in the Trojan horse or drawing a cabbage. What is important is the shared experience between student and children, the respect for each other's point of view, and the kind of language work that will best help the children to make sense of their experience.

Mrs. Rosen's article makes it clear that the teacher's role requires sensitivity and resourcefulness in engaging with children. She describes the process whereby, typically, her students move towards acquiring these qualities mainly through work with children, followed by discussion and reflection. At the beginning of this book, Professor Britton and Miss Martin gave us an account of language which shows it to be the means to integrate a child's learning right across the curriculum: the following article puts forward some of the principles, founded in this sort of account, that should underlie the whole of a student's training for teaching.

LANGUAGE IN THE INITIAL TRAINING OF THE PRIMARY SCHOOL TEACHER

Anthony Jones

> 'Students leave college these days not knowing anything
> about the teaching of reading!'
> 'Why don't the colleges get down to the job of teaching
> these youngsters the basics!'

These common cries of criticism, often based on a utilitarian misunderstanding of the problem, and the frustration of schools that have no satisfactory language policy, do, in fact, highlight a fundamental weakness in the training of teachers: *we do not attend adequately to the development of students' sensitivity to language nor to their skill in using it.* If we attend to language at all, we do so in ways least likely to be effective, in odd fragments of the time-table where practices are preached that are denied or ignored in other fragments of the student's course. In some colleges, one hears, such language work as there is consists of a series of lectures delivered to several hundred students at a time: what possible relevance can this kind of teaching have for young people who will need to teach through the medium of language used in intimate and personal contact with children? Another typical arrangement is for groups of 20-30 students to have some 40 weekly meetings, spread over two years, with their English tutor. If performance in school practice is anything to go by, we should be unwise to rate very highly the influence and effectiveness of our teaching on these courses. Some students get from them a few isolated ideas for creative writing, which they use if their supervisor and the school are that way inclined; a few pick up some information about children's literature, but often one finds them using the least demanding story they can find as an end-of-the-day soporific; those that decide to have a shot at some drama may well use the *Peter and the Wolf* they did in Physical Education, or they will go over the mime lessons from elocution courses they attended before coming to college. In other words, students will leave college with a rag-bag of time-filling exercises *for the children*, emphasizing the gulf between the teacher who knows, who provides, who criticizes, and the child who is exercised and assessed. This is a poor substitute for what the young teacher needs —an awareness of language as the main medium by which we come to terms with and share significant experience.

If we consider the uses to which students put their mother tongue on their three-year course we find too little that is relevant, too much that is inimical, to their future roles either as primary school teachers or as social beings. Students have to be too much concerned with matters outside their experience, with matters that would be more appropriate study for teachers with five years' classroom experience. They spend weary hours listening to, and bandying back and forth in discussion, words, words, words—empty, and unrelated to fact or fantasy. For them, language becomes increasingly abstract, generalization divorced from living. Students' written work, which should be exploring and ordering both past and new experience, making it part of themselves, consists mainly of summaries of facts and ideas taken from secondary—and often second rate—sources. A colleague has estimated—perhaps inaccurately—that more than 90 per cent of the writing done in colleges of education is generalization, opinion, assertion, unrelated to concrete, specific experience, and compares this with the post-graduate paper in the learned journal, where one would expect only a tiny proportion of modest generalization arising from specific evidence. I am not offering the learned paper as a model for the writing of student teachers—it is often too impersonal—but merely indicating that much of the academic work of the colleges is misguided. Nor am I saying that college of education students are more opinionated and assertive than post-graduates—I am sure that this is not the case—only that they are constantly being asked to write about matters they cannot possibly know, in any real sense of the word, and have not the time or the facilities to get to know;

198

so they produce words for assessment, to meet their commitments.

While teaching in colleges of education I have had occasional glimpses—only occasional, only glimpses—of situations in which there seemed evident a dynamic development in individuals and in groups, and in which the use of language and other expressive media had purpose, variety and depth. Oddly enough, these occurred mostly in 'introductory' courses which the students went through during their first few weeks in college. On one occasion, four lecturers were apportioned about 30 students (seven/eight each) and given freedom to plan a fortnight's course for them. The college staggered its start to the year so that commitments to other groups were light during this fortnight. Three of the lecturers were involved in the planning of the course—one from Art, one from English, and one from French. We were subsequently joined by a historian who took his students off to look at the local church's vestments. The college is in an industrial town, so we planned to spend the fortnight getting to know an industrial environment—we called the project 'Factory Life'. I will try to summarize this course in a few sentences, although an understanding of the basic, rather obvious, principles is what is most relevant to my argument: we had an uninterrupted and extended period of time to get to know something at first hand, and to work on our personal impressions; we had the experience of working with other people and giving shape and significance to aspects of our experience in several media. The course had the added excitement that its content was living material, not dead. Inevitably, the first morning of the course was given over to mass lectures to the whole year group on such subjects as 'Exploring the Environment' and 'Learning through Experience', but for the rest of the fortnight our students worked either on their own, or in seminar groups of seven or eight with their tutor, or in their group of thirty. We visited a coal mine, a mill, a nylon spinning plant, a pottery (not everyone went everywhere); we read some Alan Sillitoe and D. H. Lawrence; we saw a film about a French industrial town; a factory safety officer came

199

to college and talked to us about the human and technical sides of his job; we spent an afternoon on a mountain away from it all. Perhaps we laid on too much, but the students still had a lot of freedom to make their own explorations, to talk to people in the market, in shops, in the fish and chip queue, in pubs, to visit the library, the art gallery and churches of various denominations, and to go to a professional football match. One day we took over the art and craft studios by arrangement, and the students (few of whom had had previous experience to speak of) did some very satisfying work in two and three dimensions based on what they had seen, thought, felt and collected on the course—including, incidentally, impressive sculptures in welded metal made up of materials collected in the scrap yards. Everybody did some writing during the course, and this work—stories, poems, reporting, etc.—was transferred to tape. When we listened to these tapes on the last day they gave rise to heated, at times angry, controversy, and it was obvious that we needed more time to pursue, and try to understand, the divisions that had arisen in the group over their writing: we had had the experience 'but missed the meaning' as T. S. Eliot puts it. But even if we discount these divisions, it does not take very much imagination to see that such a fortnight's work might bring to the surface a number of interests that would provide a basis for study and creative work during many weeks to come—which in our case (as, I suspect, in most comparable cases) we had not got. The group was scattered, and, as some would say, 'got down to the serious work of the course'.

This 'Factory Life' project offers only a glimpse of some of the priorities and principles which should inform the planning and running of courses of initial training for primary and middle school teachers. It is not offered as a blue-print: I do not necessarily see the three/four year courses as a succession of environmental studies, although I am sure that these, accompanied by plenty of work with children and a full programme of reading, would provide a better training than a good deal of what happens at the moment. But before leaving the example of this project it is worth considering more closely the place of a particular day's work in such a context. I have shown how the experience of an industrial town found expression in a day's art. On another occasion, on another similar course, we arranged a drama day. Among other things, we had studied archive material of the unhappy Pentrich revolution, and during the drama day we worked on this material in a variety of very searching ways. Although on these art and drama days we worked within the terms of specific disciplines, the expression on each occasion gained depth and purpose from its context.

I have had other glimpses of a way of working that, properly developed, might get nearer to the heart of the job of initial training than we normally do. I took ten students into a school and, using two classes, we worked with children for a half day every week, more or less throughout the year. By a coincidence, some of the students were also in an English group which I met once a week in college and we were able to use material arising out of the school work in lectures. We worked with the children in small groups and as whole classes. This half day a week arrangement proved unsatisfactory in a number of ways: the only time we had together to discuss what we were doing, and what we were going to do next, was at the end of the afternoon or morning of the teaching session—when we were tired and hungry and a little bit glazed over. (Hunger, fatigue, family problems and the like often mock such desirable notions as continuity, involvement and expressiveness.) We were harried by the school's ancillary workers. The students had a packed time-table and many other commitments so that preparation for teaching was often too hurried and superficial. A few hours' contact per week with a group of children does not make for the satisfactory relationship necessary to the kind of work we were trying to do. We had not properly learned the knack of involving the class teachers in the teaching or the training of the students. There was no opportunity to relate the insights gained in this contact with children to wider conceptual frameworks—at this stage of their training,

I am not sure that this was a very serious matter. (Come to that, the students may well have been having lectures in Child Development, Sociology, Psychology and Educational Philosophy, but if they were, then I knew nothing about it, and saw no evidence that they were making connections.) But here, clearly, was the basis of what might have been even more valuable training than we in fact were able to give ourselves: we needed more time to discuss the work, to assemble, prepare and evaluate material, and to do work at our own level which would interpenetrate what we were doing with children. In any event, this was a co-operative venture, students and experienced teachers working together with children, and when we did find time to discuss we were able to give some shape and purpose to matters in which we were all involved.

F. D. Fowler has written:

> Men are neither philosophers nor poets to begin with but creatures who have to cooperate to get the mere necessities of life. Language is a social invention and man could not live in society without it. Without attempting to establish a theory of the origin of language, we can reasonably doubt accounts which overlook the primary role of verbal behaviour in enabling human beings to act together. I cannot believe that either the word or the concept had priority over the cooperative behaviour itself. (*Language and Education*, p. 37, Longman.)

In his tentative chronology of the word and the flesh, Mr. Flower could lead us into theological quicksands, but what is surely true is his statement of the primal relationship that exists between acting together and language. Our educational ethos works against co-operation: its emphasis is on individual effort towards a standardized end; it is competitive, for there are only so many places, so many passes, and so many firsts. (Reactionary tracts are not voices crying in the wilderness but express the influence that is still dominant in our school system.) But the mutual stimulation, support and enrichment of resources that result from shared enterprises and experiences, are recognized in much primary and secondary teaching, and find an increasing place in industry, the arts, therapy, research, and so on. Co-operative enterprise that is imaginatively and intellectually demanding must be an important feature of initial training.

It is likely, and surely desirable, that specialist teaching, in some form or another, will continue to be part of the student's initial training. Thus, if enlightened language work is to be the core of this training, and to pervade it at every point, then it is essential that specialist lecturers give fresh thought to the way that students exploit their natural language resources in working on their subjects, and to the positive contribution that specialist study can make to the student's language resources. Language is too important to be left entirely to the English lecturer: indeed, when he looks at the laboratories and workshops, at the trained perception of the environment available to other specialists, the English lecturer sometimes feels that the devil has all the best tunes, the facilities to teach English as it often should be taught.

In many ways, especially through Nuffield Science and Mathematics, and more especially in the primary school, subject specialists have done a great deal towards forcing a breakthrough in the teaching of the mother tongue. Particularly, we are now more conscious of the continuity that there is between what we once thought of as creative or imaginative work on the one hand, and practical uses of language on the other: we see that all varieties of language grow from what Frank Whitehead has called an 'undifferentiated matrix'. A freer mode of expression can produce work that is intellectually more vigorous—better science, not worse. (The odd thing is that Nuffield Science seems to have become an autonomous subject, separate from other sciences.) Yet, in the middle and lower secondary schools, the subject disciplines weigh heavily against integrated studies, the interests and emotional needs of children, and the development of expressive activities, because examiners are slow to revise their demands, and appear to steer teaching methods to the production of standardized answers presented in the restricted conventions of their specialism. As in the schools, so in the colleges: language can be crushed and distorted or stimulated and fostered in the areas of specialist teaching. (Among these, incidentally, I would include literature, drama, linguistics and the sub-disciplines of faculty Education, as well as all the other 'subjects'.)

I should like to look briefly at language in operation in one area of specialist study—the scientific disciplines —which I single out only because I have had some recent (very enjoyable) experience of teaching English to science students. John Dixon summarizes the demands that scientific study makes on language resources:

> In scientific disciplines too the preliminary observations, the exact framing of hypotheses (and the choice between them), and the elaboration of verifying experiments, all involve language. Such language operates at several levels of abstraction, from the simplest one of playing a role in the selection of relevant material from the mass of all that is observed, to the complex levels that permit a critical awareness of the conceptual framework to which the hypothesis relates. (*Growth through English*, p. 67, O.U.P.)

One cannot, however, expect children, or students in colleges of education for that matter, to enter a laboratory and switch entirely from the expressive language of common experience to the special conventions of scientific statement. In *Language, The Learner and the School* (Penguin), James Britton has reproduced—from a film made by the Nuffield Science Project—conversations of a class of twelve-year-old children who have been heating copper on a flame. The children talk in small groups and then all together as a class. There are several pages of transcript (which I have not the space to reproduce here) and it seems to me that this talk is not a special language, and differs from random conversation only in its spareness, which is imposed by the task in hand, and the fact that the teacher is nudging it, fairly unobtrusively, towards constructive thought. The first phase of the talk is concerned with finding and formulating possible explanations for the copper's turning colour. Professor Britton comments:

> I believe ... that the movement in words from what might *describe* a particular event to a generalization that might *explain* that event is a journey that each must be capable of taking for himself—*and that it is by means of taking it in speech that we learn to take it in thought.*
> The second phase is the mustering of the alternative explanations, and, from there, the devising of means to verify them....

Referring to the specific formulations of scientific statement that emerge from the less disciplined language of speculation, Britton concludes his comments on this transcript:

> The spare look this language has may mislead us into thinking that it can easily be learnt. But the task is not that of learning a language; rather it is that of acquiring, *by the agency of the language*, the ability to perform these mental operations I have been talking about. *A child's language is the means*: in process of meeting new demands—and being helped to meet them—his language takes on new forms that correspond to the new powers as he achieves them. Expressive speech is one of the more accessible forms; the language of scientific hypotheses, spare though it may appear, comes later.

Although these Nuffield children do not always say the right thing, what they say clearly has a meaning for themselves and their listeners. It sometimes seems to me that as children advance up the educational ladder, what they say, and certainly what they write—especially in connection with their studies—means less and less to them. In fact, I suspect that there are times when what a student writes will mean more to the teacher who taught him than it will to him. I recently asked some science students to take it in turns to talk to the group about some topic—preferably a scientific one—which interested them. For some reason or other I thought that they would go to good quality scientific journalism for their material, probably because I saw the assignment as one which would stimulate discussion at the level of the educated layman, for most of them were articulate and expressive people. But in the event, the majority, I suspect, went back to their A level courses—and probably their A level notes. With one or two exceptions, to deliver these talks they retreated into a kind of capsule of stiff, inflexible language, dense with technical terms. At the conclusion of one talk I asked if there was anything the rest of the group didn't understand or disagreed with? No, it was all perfectly clear and correct. Very good, in fact. Well I didn't understand it, I read out a list of all the words I had never heard before, and those I had heard but didn't know the meaning of. Was it possible to put the information in a simpler way so that I could get some inkling of its meaning? How could I expect to understand it, they said, if I hadn't done A level? But I understand chemical compounds. That's O level stuff, they said, and things are different at A level. I asked them if they could explain a particular term to me, like 'ion', or to explain what was the significance of ionization, anyway. Gradually, one or two began to try to reformulate parts of the information, or to link it up with things that might be within my existing knowledge, such as the working of my body cells. When they began to break into the set pattern of language symbols that had been presented to us, and to relate it to a framework of reference, they began to disagree with and contradict one another. They understood and agreed with one another only as long as the information was formulated in a certain way. Science is like that, they said, not a lot of waffle like English, it means what it says and nothing else, and you can't twist it about. It seemed to me that the language, and other symbols, with which they were representing this knowledge to themselves was actually obscuring the meaning for them—and, more than that, giving them the illusion that they understood. They were undergoing a linguistic mirage, in fact.

But, even so, the students' difficulty in communicating some advanced science was as real as mine in understanding, and would have taxed experienced teachers. We explored the possibility of using analogy to explain the process of ionization (we had got as far as seeing that we were trying to explain a process as much as a substance—I don't know if we were right). They were, in fact, very inventive, but thoroughly dissatisfied with this exercise: they thought that images of little men getting on and off buses and buses driving into garages not only were frivolous, but probably distorted the truth. Was it not better to have a distorted but concrete truth than an abstract mystery? The danger in this, apparently, is that you cannot go on to the next stage of learning if your version of the last one is personal: they seemed to see scientific learning, anyway, as a construct of well fitting standardized parts. I must confess that I am not competent to challenge this view, nor to say how ion should be described (although I am sure it is necessary to know what difference, if any, its presence or absence makes to our existence), nor whether it was appropriate to teach it at all in the A level course. Certainly I have found that Faraday in *The Chemical History of the Candle*, and Lorenz in *King Solomon's Ring*, make scientific processes and concepts accessible to a layman, and, while there may be a limit to the value of this kind of language to a scientist, I am sure that their means of expression is much nearer to the language that children and students need to use in coming to terms with new knowledge and ideas.

Harold Rosen, in his article 'The Language of Textbooks' (*Talking and Writing*, Methuen) has said of the way that many textbooks are written that their language 'looks at children across a chasm'. He goes on:

> The worst way to bridge this chasm is to encourage children to take over whole chunks of it as a kind of jargon. (Examinations have been the great excuse.) For fluent children, such as moderately successful grammar school pupils, this process is fatally easy. Probably few of us who have grown up in the system are free from some taint of this

schooling. Instead of the new formulations representing hard-won victories of intellectual struggle or even partial victories, they are not even half-hearted skirmishes. Instead, there is empty verbalism, sanctioned utterance and approved dogma; behind them is a void or a chaos. The personal view is made to seem irrelevant; it is outlawed. The conventions of this language are not taken over as are the conventions of other uses of language, at first experimentally and then with growing confidence, but unthinkingly, lock, stock and barrel. Language and experience have been torn asunder.

My science students left me one day knowing less about DNA than when they arrived. This was not my intention at all, yet I am sure that it should be a function of all teaching in the colleges to encourage students to question the formulations of their knowledge, and to work over the experience from which the formulations are derived in different ways. The teaching of new 'subjects' such as Psychology, Philosophy, and Sociology should, at its own pace, take root in the undifferentiated, expressive language of the students. We should not try to cover so much, and we should have the students work on the material in a way that makes it their own. The use of expressive, and even poetic, modes of language in specialist teaching could make the intellectual engagement with new material more genuine and purposeful, not less.

This article has dealt so far mainly with the students' own experience of language, especially in its expressive and referential modes. How important is it—how far is it possible—for the student to know *about* language? Certainly students need to spend a lot of time studying talk and writing of every kind (especially that used by children), but the purpose of this will be to extend awareness of, and sharpen insight into, language events. I doubt if we give enough time to this practical study of language, which I am sure is more valuable than the study of linguistic theory in a void.* But at the very

---

* Cf. 'Classroom Encounter' in which Connie Rosen explains how she aims a linguist at her students when they are up to their elbows in their own experiences of language work with children.

least we need criteria for selecting our 'texts', and some theory will help us with our insights. 'The linguistic theories have not yet caught up with the needs of teachers because of the present speed of change.' (Dixon quoting John Sinclair)—and because of this uncertainty I believe that we are entitled to do some cautious dabbling in a variety of theories that offer tentative answers to such questions as: what is happening when we listen, talk, read and write? How do spoken and written language differ, and what have they got in common? How does language vary with the purposes for which we use it? How does language vary according to such factors as class, occupation, geographical region, etc.? What kinds of switches are we required to make in moving from one variety to another? What is correct and what appropriate usage? How does the course of history affect language? What relationship does language have to meaning and situational context? How much language are we born with? How do we acquire it? Through what stages and by what processes do we develop and deteriorate in language performance?

Dixon sees language study as a means of freeing the student from disabling concepts of language and helping him to know what it is to be human. More particularly, it can be a means of making him more sympathetic, sensitive and resourceful in dealing with children.

To return to my glimpses. In considering ways in which initial training can offer students vital language experience, one *might* concentrate one's attention on the courses that English departments run for all students—variously known as General, Basic and Curriculum English courses. Many students—and this is especially true in my experience of students who have had a break between school and college—find these courses refreshing and broadening, and sometimes useful in terms of practical teaching. As things stand at the moment, English lecturers may well be justified in deciding that the limited time available to them should be devoted to working on the students' personal experience and preoccupations, and giving them a rare lift into the world of the imagination: many students may get little chance in the rest of their course for using language (to use James Britton's terms) in the role of spectator, and in its expressive and poetic modes; if the English lecturer pushes story, poetry and 'creative' writing, then perhaps a few students will be inspired to carry the torch into the classroom. The trouble with this view of the English course is that it works towards a separation of expressive and poetic language from referential; it can appear to by-pass the claims of basic literacy, and, indeed, to leave the 'basics' (as they so often are in practice) empty of personal meaning. To the student, 'creative English' is seen as a departmental commodity fighting for attention among other departmental commodities, whereas language should be the central, unifying factor in his training, and *his way of working* should make him aware of the continuum of experience that runs through, say, the child telling his teacher about his gran falling downstairs, the child writing down the names of the people he knows as part of the process of learning to read and write, the child writing an account of digging clay from a nearby ditch and modelling with it, a discussion of Anna's victorious dance in *The Rainbow*, a group improvisation of a discotheque scene, an illuminating article in a scientific journal, and a major artist shaping and projecting his vision through the medium of a novel, a poem, a play or a film. Furthermore, it is essential for the primary school teacher to relate his language to work in other expressive arts— movement and design—and drama will be an inevitable component of his English.

While colleges continue to organize their curricula departmentally, it seems to me that we need to allocate more time, with more continuity, for English—even if this means augmenting the English staff with people from other departments. But I think that the real answer is to review the curriculum of the colleges of education, and to see it in a fresh perspective. At the moment we look at the curriculum—whenever we do see it whole—from the apex of a departmentalized institution, when we should be seeing it from the standpoint of a talented and creative class teacher. One needs to create conditions where the very best kind of teaching can take place:

the student needs the opportunity for contact with the outside world, to break through the cordon sanitaire that so often insulates academic life in school and college; he needs plenty of contact with children, teachers and parents. Most of all, students need the opportunity to get involved and absorbed in what they are doing, to work on their material and their own experience without interruption. The time-table should be organized so that students *can work on a single task, or one set of integrated tasks, over an extended period of time*: in this way we are able to carry our work to a more satisfying depth and commitment. At the moment, many students, during any given week, will nod in the direction of half a dozen or more bodies of knowledge and types of skill; we should be delighted and astonished that many do more than make such appropriate noises as will serve to get them by.

It is impossible, unfortunately, in the scope of this article to produce a detailed plan of the kind of pattern that would satisfy the requirements we have suggested, but I can set out some of the principles that should govern such a plan:

1. We must first of all give up the attempt to provide every student with departmental teaching in a large number of subject areas—especially within the compass of any one week's timetable.
2. We should reduce the student's areas of work to two —professional studies on the one hand and academic/ creative work on the other. In practice, most college tutors would teach in both areas, and we should work in ways that related one to the other.
3. The student's professional training should (a) be integrated under the tuition of a small team of inter- (or non-) departmental tutors. (b) It should recognize certain essential priorities—such as the centrality of the mother tongue to learning and growth, and the importance of mathematics to life in the modern world. (c) We should conduct our professional training in such a way that the student will encounter and use a variety of materials and activities that will enrich children's development. (We should carry the principle of the dissolution of subjects

211

into practice.) (d) Professional studies should be school based, as far as this is practicable, and should dovetail with work at the student's level in college. (e) Sub-disciplines of faculty Education would be taken out of the area of professional studies, and made available to students among the academic/creative areas of study.

4. The student's three years' training would be divided into a series of units (perhaps nine, conforming with the present terms, but the number and size of the units could vary). Each unit would consist of *either* professional *or* academic/creative studies, and the student would work *in only one unit at a time*. During his course the student would do units from both professional and academic/creative areas, but it would be possible for him to have some say in the number of units of each kind that he tackled, so allowing some to do more academic/creative work, some more professional work, than others. This would face up to the fact that students differ in the ways that they learn, and adapt themselves to, a professional role: some express themselves, and so prepare themselves, through scholarship and creative work, some through more extensive and immediate involvement with children's learning and the teacher's arts. Both are valid, given careful selection and tutorial guidance: the opportunity to choose the emphasis in one's training must surely lead to more liberating and satisfying work—to say nothing of higher standards. In a multi-professional college it would, moreover, be possible for a student to do one of his professional units in another profession.

5. A student should be able to do his units of academic/creative work in different subject areas.

I have completed this article with a view of the initial training curriculum that goes well beyond the work of the English specialist, because I think that good language work depends on factors that are often placed beyond his control. We need a way of working that takes account of the best practices of the university, the primary school, and, I suspect, all creative work situations—offering continuity, choice, and the opportunity for personal commitment to the job in hand.

The examples in the last article were taken mainly from the teaching of subjects other than English; but we could show, equally, that the teaching of Literature (whether at specialist level, or in a General English course) often fails to give students a learning experience that is appropriate either to the reading of literature or to their needs as intending teachers. The most common failing is that students are led to take over, inertly, the reading and value judgements of lecturers and critics, with the result that their own discussion (when there is any) and their writing is derivative in the bad sense, and superficial. We suggest that there are two fundamental reasons for this (both of which were dealt with in different contexts in the last article). The first is the fragmentation of the curriculum, which derives largely from a misguided and hopeless attempt to 'cover', academically, everything that might be relevant to a teacher's career: this fragmentation works against the committed reading that is necessary if one's understanding and appreciation of a text is to be rooted in one's personal response to it. (A lecturer is probably wrong to assume that his audience has an active knowledge of a given text or that his lecture comes to the students as a relevant item amid their own rich programme of reading.) The second most general weakness in literature courses is that not enough opportunity is given to students, early on, to talk over and write about their actual experience of literature; that college teachers are not sufficiently willing to recognize and accept the limited and varied experiences of the talkers and writers—the need to go over reading that has been important, moving, puzzling, unsatisfying, the need for talk that begins from such standpoints as, 'When we did *Macbeth* at school for O level, the teacher ...', 'The only bit of Shakespeare I ever really enjoyed ...', 'That reminds me of my grandfather when ...', 'Why has everybody got a down on Enid Blyton?', '*Redgauntlet*'s boring, I couldn't get past the first few pages ...', 'It's quite good to start with, but then it seems to go off a bit ...'. Discussion of this kind needs to be in small groups; and if the lecture programme has to be reduced to make it possible, there will be no loss and almost certain gain. It is sometimes thought that, as students advance in their English course, they need fewer lectures. But there is a strong contrary case, that they ought not to be exposed to lectures until they can stand up to them —that is, until, in small groups, they have discovered their voices and the validity of their own experience and responses, however underdeveloped.

If one thinks of the fact that children's attitudes to literature, the pleasure and value that they take from stories and poems, their notion of what literature *is*,* are significantly influenced—often critically—by teachers who have no specialist interest, then the sort of contact with literature such teachers have as students takes on a considerable importance. The complacency of the Plowden Report in its section on 'Poetry' is quite inept. Thus it tells us:

> Some good teachers lack conviction about the value of poetry...

implying that the great majority of good teachers are readers of poetry for their own pleasure, since this *can* be the only basis for 'conviction'. The general air is of wanting not to know, of suggesting vaguely that everything is not too bad really and moving slowly towards being very good indeed. *Immediately after* a paragraph containing, not pessimisms, but the (very debatable) statement:

> The number of really good anthologies for children ... has increased rapidly in the last few years.

as well as the comfortable reference to some good teachers lacking conviction, we are told:

To leave an account of literature and poetry here would be to present too pessimistic a picture. There is some evidence that the tide is beginning to turn.

Surely that last image cannot be intended to be taken precisely? The following may be true:

The proportion of young teachers who are sensitive to quality in literature, and knowledgeable about children's books, seems to be increasing.

but what increase is being suggested, roughly? The point of the statement, in its context, is that it should not provoke that kind of retort. Unavoidable phrases, such as 'a growing number of schools' and 'seems to be increasing', too easily express the corporate voice of the inspectorate attempting to please everybody. Accommodation is the voice's characteristic mannerism:

Poetry written for adults, or written at least by those who are poets in their own right, is usually to be preferred to children's verse.

When isn't it preferable? But again, the question is inappropriate, since the purpose of the whole section is to *relax* attention.

The section does have its moments of realism:

But a teacher can only share with children what he understands and likes. He can only choose wisely what to share when he has both a well developed critical sense and an understanding of children.

It is a pity that the writers of the Report chose not to make explicit some of the practical implications of this view. Unless this sort of job is tackled, a situation is perpetuated whereby laudable general principles and aims actually get in the way of their own realization; for reference to them merely promotes a complacency that

215

obscures what is not achieved, so that insufficient attention is given to possible ways of bringing about improvement. With this in mind, we offer the following sketch
of what we take to be the minimum requirements in the
training of all teachers who may find themselves responsible, in some degree, for taking literature with children.

Teachers, even English specialists, often seem to regard
literature, simply, as 'material' for the classroom. When
they read a poem to themselves, or discuss it with a
colleague, there is a tendency for it to be sieved, from the
start, through a concern with how it might 'go', how it
could be *used.* This, it seems to us, is to short-circuit
the proper process which should include a stage in which
the teacher reads just for himself. Only as a result of this
can he know fully what he thinks of the poem, which
knowledge is essential to an adequate notion of why
he wants to put it before children—reaching it is a
necessary preliminary to speculations about how
children's reactions would differ from his and why
nevertheless he would like to present the poem to them,
and to decisions as to how he should go about this.

That (*pace* the Plowden Report) almost all children's
anthologies are at best mediocre can be seen as a symptom of the common failure to recognize this;* and so
can the practice of regarding poems as decorative adjuncts
to the stuff of real work ('sugar on the pill') or no more
than 'starting points'. The latter suggests a fear that
there can't be enough in a poem to engage children on
its own terms; that reading and perhaps discussing a
poem is not enough—one must always *do* something with
it, and the more activities that can be connected with it,
the better. Now it will often happen that a reading of
a poem leads naturally to work that is not essentially *of*
it, or that some occasion or activity makes the reading
of a particular poem especially apt; but to say that is
to register little more than that poems are *about* things—
things that don't exist only in poems (though many
anthologists, in the vacuity of their choices, come close

---

* Cf. page 116 above.

216

to implicitly denying this); it does not preclude a recognition that there are gains to be had from poetry as poetry—from the *ways* of representing the world, and the meanings peculiarly generated thereby, that are termed 'poetic' (and which are subsumed in James Britton's more general category).

The limitation of children's conceptions of poetry,* and hence of what they gain from it, is largely caused by teachers with very limited and misguided notions of what constitutes poetry and its relevance to life. It is worth noting here that, because a teacher enjoys poetry, it does not necessarily follow that he is free of such notions. However, it seems safe to say that most harm is done by the majority of teachers who have little or no respect, of any kind that can be called genuine, for poetry. Such an assertion, with its reference to 'the majority',† need not appear gratuitous if 'respect' is carefully defined. What 'respect' entails, minimally, is an understanding that poetry is not to be toyed with; that if poetry 'can be fun', it is important that the 'fun' be not such as to induce in children preconceptions that will serve to alienate them, totally or partially, from other poetry when they meet it thereafter; that if poetry is to be used by teachers who would not think of reading it outside a classroom or without a classroom in mind, it should not be used carelessly; that although no one can possibly be blamed for not having a comprehensive and developed appreciation of poetry, that is no reason to act as if such a lack were of no consequence.

Three implications of what we have just been saying, for the training of teachers, are as follows. First, it is important that students have as many opportunities as possible to read and discuss poetry at their own level. Secondly, not only should their teachers follow the principles we outlined at the beginning of this note, but they should be explicit about this, and promote discussion

---

* See 'Writing Poetry in the Classroom' above.

† We should emphasize that we have non-specialists particularly in mind.

about what sort of activity the reading and discussion of literature should properly, though variously, be. Thirdly, pedagogical considerations should arise out of, not precede or bypass, such discussion (this should be seen as complementing the basic general principle that students cannot have too much contact with children). We see the minimal practical objectives of talking about poetry as the recognition that, if one does not enjoy poetry, it might well be better not to take it at all with children (but at least to make sure that they have ready access to books of poems which other teachers, who do have a serious interest in poetry, recommend); if one's enjoyment sticks at, say, nursery rhymes and chanting games,* one should be conscious, albeit without much precision, of the dangers of giving children a limited diet in such a way as to condition their expectations debilitatingly.

Much of what we have said in the last few paragraphs applies to fiction as well as to poetry. We referred there specifically to poetry because it focusses the problems most sharply; student teachers are much more likely to arrive at college with a resistance to poetry than to stories. However, we certainly would not suggest that an attempt should be made to coerce students into an enjoyment of poetry (it would inevitably fail). Moreover, it would be important to adapt arrangements to the needs, not of each student (which would usually be impracticable) but of different *kinds* of student: for example, the resistance of some students to poetry might be dissolved by talking about fiction (both for adults and for children, and in either case without the classroom in mind initially) first.

There would be little point in our suggesting what fiction and poetry, and how much, it would be appropriate for students to study, without these suggestions being incorporated in an extended case for the study of literature that would be out of place in this book. Besides,

---

* Nursery rhymes and chanting games can, of course, be very valuable: see 'A Dragon Can Be a Gift' above.

we think that decisions ought as much as possible (and increasingly throughout the course, whether specialist or General) to be made collaboratively, by teachers and students. But perhaps it should be noted that whereas there is depressingly little poetry written for children that is worthy of them, there are now many works of fiction, written for children and which children enjoy, that can be rewarding to adults even if they have no pedagogical designs upon them. Any General English course that did not create many opportunities for students to discover this fact would seem to us to be failing in its priorities. For this discovery—of the continuity of children's fiction at its best and good adult fiction; of the superiority of some children's fiction to much adult fiction—can help significantly to increase the seriousness with which teachers tackle the business of what to put before children. Primarily, though, such seriousness (as in all pedagogical matters) will be a function of understanding children; how they are similar to, and how they differ from, adults—and each other. At the most general level, this is the burden of the present book.

||||||||||||||||||||||||||||||||||||||||||||||||||||||||||||||||||||||||||||||||||||||||||||||||||||||||||||||||||

POSTSCRIPT

What it all adds up to is one way of looking at things. One way of interpreting to ourselves what we have seen and heard and done in schools—in and around schools, rather—and in and around colleges of education. There are of course other ways of looking, other interpretations of the place of language in these institutions.

Clearly, we can never be happy about what goes on in schools, in general, so long as we are unhappy about what goes on in general in colleges of education. There is no shortage of problems. Yet we know the cart from the horse: what goes on in colleges of education today must stand or fall by its effect upon children in school tomorrow. And so this book, while seeing the two problems in close relationship, is above all a book about schools and schoolchildren. (And that—to take it on the rebound—is one of the things that we believe a college of education course must certainly be.)

Yes, there are other views: so that in a sense we are, as editors, writers, committee members, 'standing up to be counted'. We can claim little courage for the act, however, since we believe ourselves to be part of a long slow revolution that started at least as far back as John Dewey: a revolution that is slow in the very process of defining its policies since policy, by its insistence, must be born of successful practice.

What seems relatively clear at the moment is that our view of the role of language in Primary education has two implications that deserve the adjective 'revolutionary'. The first is an attack on the traditional relationship of teacher to taught, and the second an attack on traditional notions of what constitutes 'learning'. Both implications have been much misunderstood and therefore resisted for the wrong reasons; both are vulnerable because still abounding in problems and hedged around by uncertainties. In a successful classroom—any among hundreds today—each is demonstrated with conviction to anyone whose experience—however inadequately analysed, if at all—has prepared him to recognize it.

220

I need not labour the matter of the relation between teacher and taught since it has been referred to more or less directly in all the preceding sections. Very simply, we have to recognize that we stand as one individual human being to another in our relations with the children we teach. It is not 'given to us' to teach them whether they will or no, for that is an impossibility. It may of course be our responsibility to 'police' them for the protection of other children or for our own, but teaching and learning can begin only where that leaves off. Even upholders of an authoritarian teacher's role, in looking back, will sometimes refer to highly influential moments in their own school careers and in doing so illuminate moments of generosity and humility—rare enough perhaps—on the part of their teachers: generosity in giving from their greater wisdom and experience, humility in doing so without demanding payment in psychic currency—acquiescence, respect, gratitude or any other mark of subservience. It is above all in the speech of teacher and taught that the roles of trust and mutuality are established and maintained. And it is certainly easier to establish such relationships when the teacher's voice falls into place among the many voices of the children in a variety of speaking situations—teacher and child, teacher and children, child and child, and so on—rather than sounding forth in an unvarying teacher/class set-up.

As for the attack on traditional notions of what constitutes learning, I cannot make much of it here. I should need either more time or greater ability, or both, to put the philosophical argument that might begin to establish our point. Yet it is an important one: if the teacher is to yield up his power as society's plenipotentiary (or sergeant instructor in the regiment of adults), can he not fall back upon the power of his superior knowledge and wisdom? Or putting the point more honestly, what is wrong with *instructing* for the obvious purpose of ensuring that what is known to this generation is not lost to the next? And if we see anything wrong with it, are we in fact asking the teacher to abdicate altogether?

It is probably all a matter of understanding the relationship between knowledge and the knower. There are, I believe, electronic teaching machines that can engage in simple didactic dialogue with the learner. We might go on from that to conceive of an argument between two computers. Perhaps there will be computers that can handle, in more complex ways than man himself, man's most subtle formulations of what he knows. Yet what the computers manipulated would be less than 'knowing' as a man knows: and I cannot conceive that the outcome of the computer's manipulations could have any value until men took it and used it: and in doing so they would be contributing the personal, the unformulated, the intuitive aspects of knowing that cannot enter a formulation, that cannot exist apart from the individual man who knows.

In daily life we draw constantly upon other people's knowledge and wisdom: all living is such an interchange, an economy of giving and receiving. But in school, traditionally, we have tried to ignore the receiving: we have thought of giving as though it might be independent of receiving; or as though receiving were a totally passive process that could always be relied upon to occur. In other words we have thought of knowledge as transferable matter: as something that existed outside and independent of the knower.

And all this is a matter of language: by his own uses of language, in speech or writing or thought, a child must find out for himself what we tell him. And when we recognize this mysterious truth and adapt our linguistic behaviour to his we are able to *give*, to turn to good account our own knowledge and wisdom. But, by the same token, we shall find our place as teachers in the general economy of giving and receiving: what we can give will be one source of a child's learning among many, and we shall need to recognize and facilitate these other sources. To do all this effectively is very far from abdicating.

Much has been said in preceding chapters about another learning task for teachers—the need to recognize and appreciate the many uses of language by which a child goes about his learning, some of them very unlike our own. Perhaps the strangest of them, from an adult point of view, is that of dramatic play. Let me add a word or two here to what Ian Burton has already said. Of course, dramatic play is something children begin to enjoy from quite an early age: it provides the framework for a whole range of representative activity, from aping their elders to turning the world upside down. For many children it is their earliest exercise in co-operating with other children, in shared activity. In school it has particular value as spectator role activity that is *social*, the corporate expression of shared feelings and shared interests. But the main reason why I do not believe we can leave it to the home or the playground lies in its value as *exploration*. It is the form of spectator role language that is most accessible to young children: and as such it is likely to take them further into certain strange territories than any other form. (I say certain territories because I believe there are some individual problems that are best probed by the handling of individual fantasy—whether in story telling or writing or reading.)

Dramatic speech is a recreation of speech-cum-action: the imagined situation is invoked to support and stimulate the speech. Its power to explore may be crudely illustrated from adult behaviour: if the problem we are pondering reaches a certain stage of difficulty we may need to externalize it in speaking aloud—we talk about it, preferably to someone who can listen and prompt us: in doing so we are regressing to an earlier form of language usage in order to move on towards a solution. At a further level of difficulty we may even sometimes be able to externalize further and in some way *dramatize* the problem as when we 'reconstruct the crime' or even deploy the objects on the table between us—a further regression in the means for the purpose of making further progress towards an end.

The analogy is too crude: exploration in dramatic play in school is not problem solving in this sense— it is in the spectator and not the participant role. Its effects will be upon each child's representation of the world-as-he-knows-it. Its highlight will be not logical but poetic; it represents in fact the most likely avenue by which speech in school, starting in the expressive mode will reach the poetic. And where in any group that happens—when the situation corporately imagined takes over—individual children are likely to move on from that point, individually and variously, in their own speaking and reading and writing. It can be a powerful corporate experience, as can listening to the teacher's reading; but unlike that, it calls upon children's own imaginative and co-operative production of language: and as such it is focal to a great deal of valuable language activity in the classroom.

Why all this harping on the spectator role? Well, everybody wants children to grow up able to use language to get things done—and 'everybody' includes us. But it needs a fuller understanding of the importance of language to the speaker to appreciate what is afoot when children chat about their homes, improvise a story or a homely incident, write and read stories and poems. The underlying concern here is not with getting things done, but with digesting experience—first hand or recorded or imagined—and making of it, each child for himself, one world in which he is content to live. It is a concern, in other words, for the total context into which a child—a man—must fit every new experience as it comes to him.

James Britton

OXFORD UNIVERSITY PRESS

This symposium of articles by
members of the primary schools
sub-committee of N.A.T.E.
makes contributions to a theory
—founded in our understanding
of language—which offers a
basis for work in the primary
and middle school classroom.
The matter of the book turns
on two models of language
offered by James Britton, and
includes articles on writing,
drama, poetry, fiction,
environmental studies and
teacher training.

75p net
in UK   **ISBN 0 19 919007 0**